To call myself a groupie wou
Anytime I see Dr. David M. Schmittou's name on a new book, blog, or podcast, it finds its way to the top of my list. Dave is dedicated to diving into the challenging and sometimes uncomfortable topics to bring them to a new light. This book delivers a wealth of knowledge to any educator dedicated to finding a new way to explore assessment. Change your mindset. Change your practice. Change the world of education. Put this at the top of your list friends!

— RAE HUGHART, MIDDLE LEVEL MATH EDUCATOR IN ILLINOIS, CREATOR OF THE TEACH FURTHER MODEL, CO-AUTHOR OF "TEACH BETTER" AND THE DIRECTOR OF TRAINING & DEVELOPMENT FOR THE TEACH BETTER TEAM.

I thoroughly enjoyed this book! From the title I was hooked. I wish I had read this book prior to the year starting. It gave me such great insight into the differences of assessments, and how they are not so different at all if used in the right context. Dave has broken down all of the nuances of data in a simplistic way that will still help educators drive decision making. I am now more confident that when my superintendent asks me what data do I have to back up what I'm doing I can confidently support my decision. I encourage EVERY educator at every level to read this book, whether they are strong with data or not. Dave explains how to use assessment and data in the best vein for our kids. That's why we are here.

— MICHAEL EARNSHAW DAD, HUSBAND, PRINCIPAL, MARATHONX5, SKATEBOARDER, SPEAKER, INSPIRER, AUTHOR CO-HOST OF @PUNKCLASSROOMS

MAKING ASSESSMENT WORK FOR EDUCATORS WHO HATE DATA BUT LOVE KIDS

DAVID M. SCHMITTOU

EduMatch Publishing

CONTENTS

1

WHAT ARE WE TALKING ABOUT?

Assessment is the art of measuring students' inner thoughts by their outward behaviors.

L et me jump right into this. This book is NOT designed to teach you statistics. You will not learn how to calculate Z scores, measure standard deviations, or determine statistical significance. This book is designed to teach you how to measure student learning more accurately, and perhaps more importantly, help you understand what you are limited in measuring. When I was crafting the outline for this text, I could have easily planned for a book that would have been hundreds of pages long, but that would have completely defeated the purpose. My goal was to create a book that makes assessment manageable and meaningful. My aim was to make this book something that was easy to read and not bogged down with jargon and formulas. You will read analogies and metaphors during the first half of the book designed to shape the conversation and engage even the most reluctant among us in a conversation that scares so many. In the final chapters of the book, you will read about strategies that classroom teachers, schools, and districts can implement immediately to make an enduring impact. But, with that said, I have intentionally chosen not to write a text steeped in formulas, statistical reasoning, and analytical science. This is a book for educators, written by an educator, so I ask for your forgiveness early on if I do not address every possible implication that could arise from a conversation around assessment. I hope to make assessment easy to understand and to make the ideas presented in these pages easy to implement in any classroom.

In its purest form, assessment, as it will be used here, is an attempt to take internal knowledge and measure it with an external measure. It is really an exercise in translation. Students have understandings and misunderstandings in their heads, that we as educators try to draw out so that we can make inferences and draw conclusions. Because of this, we all must understand that [data analysis] and (assessment creation) are an imperfect science, subject to interpretation, just like any act of translation.

Each language on earth has its own subtleties and nuances. Idioms, similes, metaphors, and all forms of figurative language have their own meanings rooted in unique contexts and social histories. Teaching pronouns and verb agreement to an English speaker is done differently than it is to a speaker of Russian. Phonemic awareness is much different with Latin based alphabets, like English, than it is with languages with origins in the far-east like Japan or China. As linguists will tell you, these variations often make the pure translation between languages virtually impossible. There is always something lost in the translation. Think about how many English translations of the world's best selling book there are (The Bible): King James, New International, Living, New Living, etc.... There are an estimated 900 translations of the English Bible as scholars attempt to accurately determine the meaning of the original Greek, Hebrew, and Aramaic.

Do you remember that telephone game you used to play as a kid?

One person begins by sharing a message with a person seated nearby. That person repeats the message to another person and so on. By the time the message has been shared just a few times and translated through the lens of the multiple recipients, it has often changed dramatically from what was originally created in the mind of the initial speaker. This is what is at play with translating language and with interpreting assessment data.

What classroom assessments are designed to do is to translate thoughts, understandings, imaginations, and ideas into a form that we often try to quantify, convert to a scale score or a percentage, and then again into a letter grade. We attempt to take the electrical pulses of neurons in the brains of our students and convert them into tangible products that we then judge and analyze. As educators, we often spend the bulk of our time planning how to create the neural connections and very little time determining whether or not our plans for measuring those connections are actually any good. As a result, we often make incorrect inferences of knowledge and therefore misalign our instruction.

I am a firm believer in the concept of beginning with the end in mind. When John F. Kennedy made the goal in the 1960s to put a man on the moon in less than a decade, resources and ambitions were aligned towards that goal. Landing on the moon successfully was the goal. It was measured. We eventually did it and knew when we did. We knew how far we had to travel, and we knew when the Apollo Spacecraft was successful. By knowing where you are going, you can measure your progress in getting there.

That's what this book is all about, not space travel, but measured progress. It will serve as a reminder that all learning is a process. It is a journey. Recognizing a starting place and an intended target is extremely important, but determining progress on this journey is of paramount importance. This book will help you determine what your goals look like. It will attempt to help you discover ways to measure progress towards meeting those goals and how to further plan for continued progress.

As teachers, we are involved in a craft that is not linear. It is cyclical. Our job is not to just explicitly provide instruction, but instead to assess needs and progress. When you go to the doctor's office to try and improve your health, there are a few baseline tests that are run almost every time. Maybe your blood pressure, height, weight, and pulse are measured, but based upon other symptoms, you may be ordered to receive additional assessments as well. These assessments are used to help prescribe a focused treatment plan. Once prescribed, this plan usually also involves follow-up appointments where the fidelity of the treatment plan can be analyzed, with adjustments or enhancements developed, as a result, to further drive progress. In a doctor's office, assessment comes before treatment, as well as during the treatment process. Far too often in classrooms today, we offer universal treatments, if we are lucky, based on one assessment, without the knowledge of how to effectively progress monitor during the treatment, or even how to change course, as a result of data that indicates a failed treatment plan.

Imagine if your doctor did the same thing. From Monday through Thursday, every person who enters the office is given a little blue pill. The doctor knows that everyone who is showing up needs to get better. The doctor knows that the little blue pill was made to help people, so he infers that the little blue pill will help everyone who walks in. On Friday, the doctor gives his patients an assessment of health, perhaps measuring dexterity or reflexes. It doesn't matter that the pill was designed to help with hypertension, and is shocked to see that only a portion of the population is showing evidence of health, based on this measure. Those who are not healthy by this standard are then sent to the doctor across the hall to get a focused intervention, with the hopes that this doctor, who may or may not be trained in the specific specialty of need, can somehow stumble upon a cure, perhaps simply because he or she has fewer patients and thereby can give more time to each. This approach would never be permitted in medicine, yet this is the same practice we engage in daily within our schools. *growth needed in schools*

Teachers are brain surgeons. They are charged with molding, shaping, and forming human minds. It is our job to grow the minds of children, to develop them, and allow for cognitive health. As such, perhaps we, as educators and parents, should begin to understand how our lack of awareness in our assessment practices truly equates to educational malpractice.

I have a doctorate degree in Educational Leadership. I have accumulated well over 250 credit hours in educational course work. I teach as a college professor in the school of education at a college in the midwest. Throughout my own personal college experiences, as well as those I am lucky enough to teach, I am yet to experience a single course designed to successfully help teachers create, analyze, or infer as a result of assessments. As a former classroom teacher, the way I learned to assess was by working with my peers. What they did, I did. What they often did was whatever the teacher's edition of the textbook told them to do. We would teach Monday through Thursday, give a quiz on Friday and repeat this cycle until we "finished" a unit when a test would be given. The goal was to get through an entire textbook during the course of a school year, and we often did.

About fifteen years ago, I began to hear with more regularity the terms formative and summative assessment. I was told that there were two types of assessments we could use in our classrooms, those that should count for a grade and those that were merely practice. I learned that some assessments were designed to help the teacher, and some were designed to measure students. It was this flawed thinking that guided my own malpractice for years, inhibiting my ability to reach students to the fullest possible level. I hope this book frees you to reach your students in a way that I wasn't able to reach mine. By challenging some of what you already do and providing new insights, I want to help you ultimately meet your students where they are so that they can grow beyond where you ever dreamed of taking them before. As we go, one foundational belief will guide everything we discuss. The goal of assessment should always be to drive future performance. Assessment always precedes instruction and should never just complete it. It is the beginning of the cycle, not the end. Assessment does not fall into one of two categories. It is not summative or formative. The goal of any assessment should be to help develop future plans and goals. A quality assessment informs where you are so you can plan to get where you want. It is not one or the other.

In my current full-time position, I get paid twice a month, on the 10th and 25th. In my last job, I only got paid once a month. The total amount earned each month was basically the same, but let me tell you, trying to plan a month at a time for expenses is a lot more diffi-cult than having to create a budget fifteen days at a time. I am sure it is just a mental exercise, but my ability to not overextend myself and to ensure my outcome does not exceed my income has changed dramatically as a result of this change. Now, I can login to my bank account, online, twice a month, do a quick scan of purchases and deposits, make sure I am staying within my limits, and create short-term plans and corrections if I am off track. When I was only getting paid once a month, for some reason, my mindset was so different. By the 15th of every month, panic was setting in, and I found myself just trying to hold on. I found myself either in a defensive mode trying to hold on to whatever I had left, or I would put my head in the sand and pretend everything was alright and end up in debt by the time I got paid again.

I think in schools, many of us fall victim to one of these two mindsets as well. Maybe not with balancing our checkbooks, but instead balancing our lesson plan books. When I was a classroom teacher, I will admit, I struggled to make a learning "budget." I often just shot from the hip, spent my teaching capital on whatever I felt was needed on any given day, failed to adequately plan ahead, and after a few weeks, decided it was time to assess my progress. I would give students a test or a quiz on all I had covered and was often shocked to learn that I wasn't nearly as on track as I thought I was. Or, worse than that, I would give a test or quiz, would see amazing results, and failed to realize that those results were not part of any larger plan or aligned towards bigger goals, but simply a reflection of all I did. It would be akin to balancing my checkbook by looking at all of my new clothes in my closet, as opposed to the dollars and cents available in my bank account. I would analyze what I spent my capital on instead of my progress towards generating true wealth.

In schools today, data has become a term that reflects judgment, condemnation, and evaluation. Data has been perverted from a word that should drive reflection, progress, and growth, primarily because so many of us have chosen not to look at our accounts, but instead to look at our closets. When others bring us our statements and we see a negative balance, we get defensive and blame those who deliver the news, instead of looking at ourselves and reflecting on whether or not we spent our time and energy where it would be best served and making regular adjustments where needed.

When I run a negative balance or get an overdraft charge, I do not blame my bank. It is on me. I spent more than I had on things I probably did not need. The good news is that often I can call my bank, ask for a fee to be waived, and then make the necessary adjustments to avoid making the same mistake again. By having created a regular pattern of assessing my balance every two weeks, I am much more prone to staying within my limits and staying on track.

In your classroom or school, it is critical to put yourself on a schedule for assessing whether or not you are on track, spending your time and energy where you should, and making adjustments before it gets too late. In too many schools today, we are asking teachers to give up instructional time simply to assess students with the intent of predicting future success on another assessment. We put teachers on a prescribed pacing plan, in a scripted framework, ask for assessments three times a year, and one big assessment in the spring, without also allowing them to have the freedom to make adjustments, to deviate from what they have been doing and to better align their resources. We also have teachers who often do not focus on any designated plan or standards, who simply shop nightly for a new lesson idea (sometimes literally- Pinterest and Teacher Pay Teacher...ugggh). When the time comes to measure progress, they find themselves in complete shock and without a plan for how to make adjustments to what has been done or needs to be done going forward.

I am a firm believer that the secret sauce, the magic pill, the silver bullet to highly effective teaching is the ability to reflect. If teachers can determine whether or not each day has gotten them closer to a goal, whether or not students have made gains, whether or not their lesson plan book is staying balanced, without the need for a judgment laced critique, we will see amazing results. My financial adviser gives me recommendations but does not tell me what I have to do. If you are a leader of a school, the same mindset could serve you well. If you are a teacher, each month, determine how you will measure how much intellectual capital you expect your students to acquire and then spend some time at regular intervals measuring their progress. Don't wait until the end and then panic when things didn't go as planned, and don't micromanage every withdrawal. Put yourself on a pattern that allows for frequent assessment of progress coupled with the ability to make adjustments, and when judgment day does arrive, I am sure you will be in the black.

This is a book about assessment, not instruction, but I hope you can see how the two are intimately connected. A good assessment should drive good instruction, not the other way around. A good assessment is one that makes sense and that tells us the story of a child. Again, there is rarely such a thing as a good assessment or a bad assessment.

Still, there are good and bad inferences and conclusions that we can draw based upon our understanding, so let's take a closer look at some of the more common misunderstandings and try to straighten them out. We will begin with some of the terms I have already presented and will then attempt to provide a preview of some of the concepts we will discuss in later chapters.

Achievement: Typically used to describe reaching a pre-identified level of expected performance

Growth: Used to describe the progress being made towards an identified destination or target

Standard: Used to describe the primary target that will universally be assessed by all. "A standard is only standard if it is standard."

Proficiency: Often used interchangeably with "achievement," this is a definitive level of achievement that reflects mastery of a standard or collection of standards. (Note. One cannot INCREASE proficiency. Proficiency is a designated level.)

Percentages: Part of 100. Just like there are 100 cents in a dollar, a percent represents what proportion of 100 was earned or achieved. Typically this is used to represent the number of items answered correctly divided by the total number of items.

Percentiles: Also based on a part of 100, this represents where an individual ranks in comparison to 100 others. This is not based on proficiency or achievement but is used as a comparison to others. For example, a student can be the 50th percentile even if every student in a class scored between 90%-100% on a test or a student can be in the 95th percentile if every student scored between 50%-60% on a test.

Mean: Often used to describe the "average." This is calculated by determining the sum of all numbers divided by the number of items.

Median: Often used to describe the middle number. When all scores are arranged in numerical order, the score found in the middle is the median. This is sometimes helpful when determining if there are outliers* see below.*

Mode: This is used to determine the score or value that is earned most frequently. The most popular value.

Norm: Often used to describe the mean of a population* see above* or what is "normal."

Outliers: Used to describe values or scores that are a substantial distance from the norm. Using the examples from earlier, if the norm score is 62%, a score earned one time, by one student of 95% may be seen as an outlier.

Skew: The effect that outlier scores can have on determining the "average." If a student is an outlier as described above, their total score may skew the average to represent a higher score than what is accurate. This can be a problem, especially when reporting on the norm for a population.

Formative: Evidence used to inform a practice or way of thinking.

Summative: Evidence used as defining proof.

Scale scores: Often used on standardized tests, these scores are weighted to create an equal distribution along the continuum. Like inches on a ruler, the distance between scale points stays consistent, although items on an assessment utilizing scale scores are not all treated equally. For example, a student who scores a 400 may have different understandings than another student who earns a 400, but they have both acquired the same amount of understandings. (Often high order topics carry more weight and impact a scale score more than low-level recall.)

Sample: a portion of the overall population. For example, a first hour class may be a sample of all classes tested. A sample may also represent various demographic groups.

Population: all samples and subgroups combined. A population represents all people tested or all people who are attributed to a group.

Validity: the level to which we have confidence that the evidence collected measures accurately what it was intended to measure.

Reliability: the level to which we are confident that others would be able to draw the same conclusions or collect similar evidence with the same procedures.

Confirmation bias: our innate desire to skew results based on our own beliefs, opinions, and understandings.

2

DON'T LOSE SIGHT OF WHAT MATTERS MOST

If you teach a kid to learn to love your content, she will get a great test score.
If you teach a kid to love learning, she will have a great life.

It sure feels like DATA is the new four-letter word in schools. I wouldn't be surprised to walk into a faculty restroom in a school one day and find that a teacher has used a Sharpie to write those four letters onto a bathroom stall as a way to show his rebellious spirit. In some places, DATA has replaced more notorious four-letter words as the go-to for expressing displeasure. I overheard a teacher recently say she "had to go to a DATA meeting." The reaction from her coworker was similar to what I would expect if she would have used the infamous F word instead.

As educators, none of us signed up for our careers because we were fascinated by the idea of quantifying statistics and using numbers to label students. Very few of us would identify our job title as "psycho-metrician." We didn't think we were signing up to learn statistical analytics or number crunching, or at least very few of us really understood that this would become a part of our daily life. Much like a medical doctor who may enter the profession with dreams of curing chronic diseases and improving the lives of patients, who quickly learns that an essential element of the job is learning to comprehend and utilize vital statistics to properly diagnose and treat those very people he/she hopes to save, teachers and all educators must begin to gain a greater level of comprehension around at least base-level assessment. Being assessment literate is not a luxury. It is a requirement.

Pilots often choose their career path out of a desire to fly the skies and experience the freedom of movement that is not restricted by designated paths and roads. Yet, they too must understand how to calculate velocity and pitch rate to calculate their progress in meeting their goals. Even professional athletes, who often have chased their profession since childhood, are not tasked with just playing a game but are expected to understand statistical success rates. They must understand the laws of averages, basic analytics, and be able to apply these to both training and performance.

Although numbers are not why we do what we want to do as educators, if we want to do what we do at a high level, we do need to have at least a basic understanding of how they impact our kids and us. I completely understand that most other professions that require such a high level of statistical reasoning also afford a higher level of compensation, but that is something I have no control over. I am hopeful, however, that this book will at least help provide a foundation that we can all grow from. I truly believe that if you keep reading, you will gain a greater appreciation for not just numbers, but more importantly, monitoring growth and making sense of all of the data, both good and bad, that is put before you. Let's dive in.

* * *

I AM A FATHER OF FOUR AMAZING KIDS. AS I WRITE THIS, MY OLDEST IS IN middle school, and my youngest will begin preschool in the fall. Although each of my children has the same last name, each is unique and special. Each has likes, dislikes, passions, and fears. Each has strengths, and each has weaknesses. All of my children have AMAZING parents (wink, wink), but each is currently creating a life of his or her own. As my children grow up, I naturally play the comparison game. I compare my oldest child's progress to those of his peers, or even to what I remember about my own development as a child. I compare my younger three children to those who are older. I worry when developmental timeliness differs, but also celebrate when milestones are met earlier than expected.

My oldest child didn't learn to tie his shoes until he was ten years old, yet my second child was able to tie her shoes by the time she was five. Some might look at this and wonder if there was a learning delay with my oldest, preventing him from learning this skill earlier on. The answer is, yes. It was me. The fault wasn't his or a cognitive disconnect. I messed up. I decided that I was going to tie his shoes for him every morning, to simply make life easier for me...and him... and he never had to learn. By the time my daughter was born, five years later, I didn't have the same patience or time to do so, and as a result, she was able to learn earlier than her brother.

My fourth child is currently four years old, yet he is wearing the same size clothes as his six-year-old brother. When I do laundry, I cannot tell whose clothes are whose, so they simply share. The boys are roughly the same height and weight, even though almost three years separate them. They both wear the same size shirts and pants even though their ages indicate this should not be the case.

In schools, we often make judgments about students by looking at the wrong data and thereby drawing faulty conclusions. We focus too much on the calendar and not enough on the person. Assessments cannot be valid or invalid, but our inferences can be. In your school, decisions may be made by teachers or administrators because students are being compared to what is considered "normal." Labels such as "delayed" or "impaired" can be attached to a student that can last a lifetime because a skill or ability is learned at a rate or in a time period that varies from the norm.

Comparison data is often the easiest to understand so it becomes the most widely used, although, often, it is also the most harmful!

In your school or classroom, students may be expected to all be in the same phase of development because of their ages. Despite their unique growth and development, we group students together because of how many years they have been on earth and expect them to all progress at the same rate.

Gaining an understanding of how to effectively use data to determine student strengths, student opportunities, and student readiness is essential to providing quality learning experiences. Understanding data is not about turning students into numbers. It is about understanding how each student is different and how we can better respond accordingly.

A major league pitcher who walks up to the mound and thinks he will just throw a fastball past every hitter is setting himself up for failure. The great pitchers study the numbers and know which batters struggle against hitting a slider, who swings on change ups, and who can't lay off the high heat. The greats know more than who the good hitters are and who has a low average. They know how to effectively rise to the challenge of pitching not just to everyone who comes before them, but to each who comes before them. Sure there will be times when a batter defies the odds and hits one out of the park, but understanding the numbers limits those opportunities and gives the pitcher a much better chance of finding success. Understanding the difference between how to pitch to EACH and how to pitch to EVERY is the difference.

As the pitchers of academic content, it is so important that we, as educators, learn what causes our students to swing for the fences and what causes them to stand and watch an opportunity sail right by. A batter's average is not just a result of what kind of swing he has. It is also a reflection of the quality of pitching he faces.

We all want our children to find success and our ability to better understand how to assess them, how to evaluate progress, and how to target their strengths will help us do just that.

When my children were infants and toddlers, they went in for frequent "well visit" check-ups. These visits to the pediatrician were not a result of visible illnesses or ailments but were designed to analyze their health based on more than what I could observe as an untrained expert. I like to believe that nobody knows my kids better than I do, but even with that, having each of my children receive an assessment of their blood pressure, blood sugar, hearing, vision, height, weight, etc...helped me gain an even better picture on their overall well being and what I could be doing as a parent to help them grow even healthier. I was able to learn what vitamins to provide, what flexibility exercises to encourage, what vaccines to give, and could ask a multitude of questions based on the results of each test performed. My kids are not numbers, but using numbers has helped me keep them healthy, strong, and flourishing. The students in your classroom are not a summative test score. They are not an IQ. Your students are not a standard deviation from the norm. They are not a scale score or a performance level. Your students, however, deserve to have their progress monitored and evaluated. They deserve to have their intellectual and socio/emotional health measured just as they do their physical health. As experts, it is our charge to get to know each child we teach. We need to know their interests. We need to know their abilities. We need to know their weaknesses. We need to know their strengths. In some instances, it may be helpful for us to know where students compare to what is considered "normal." Still, more importantly, we must understand where each student currently is compared to their past so we can continue to propel them towards their futures. As I stated in both of my previous books (*It's Like Riding a Bike* and *Bold Humility)*, knowing the difference between reaching each student and reaching every student is the difference.

We have to create systems that allow us to focus on what a child can do, what they do know, where their strengths are, instead of focusing all of our attention on what they cannot do. A batting average is determined by calculating the number of times a player gets a hit, not how many times he failed. A player who strikes out seven out of ten times yet gets a hit three out of every ten plate appearances is not reported to have a .700 missing average, but instead a .300 hitting average. A basketball player who misses 20y of his 50 free throw attempts is not described as having a 40% miss rate but instead is reported as having a 60% free throw average. In our schools we must get away from labels such as "not-proficient," "below normal," and even big red pen marks at the top of a paper indicating the number of questions missed, and begin to focus on the level of success that has been achieved, the number of questions answered correctly.

When my kids were learning to walk, I celebrated every step they took. I did not fixate on the fact that they were not running marathons. When my kids were learning to ride their bikes, I celebrated each driveway they passed. I did not focus on the fact that they were not registered for the Tour de France. I celebrated their progress. I praised where they were, and I had realistic expectations of where I could take them. This is why assessment and the resulting feedback are so important. It is not about glorifying failure. It was, and it is, about accurately reporting quality evidence and documenting learning so that we can change the narrative from one of inadequate to one of hope. While it is important to measure both strengths and struggles, we must remember what matters most. We are defined by who we are, not by who we are not. Don't lose sight of this when assessing students. Don't define them by what they can't do. Focus on what they can.

3

LEARNING IS A PROCESS, SO WHY DON'T YOU GRADE THAT WAY?

A test cannot be valid or invalid, but the inferences we draw from them can be. The same evidence is presented in a court of law, whether you represent the plaintiff or defendant. The only difference is the inferences that are drawn from the evidence. Interpretation of evidence often matters more than the quality of evidence.

Several years ago, I hired a brand new teacher to work in my school. She was fresh out of college, full-on energy, and ready to set the world on fire. She had a great resume full of volunteer experience, great college grades, was fully certified, and had strong references. I assigned her to a classroom where she would teach middle school students, and then I sat back, ready to watch her change destinies. Unfortunately, however, her first year was not quite as flawless as I had hoped it would be. In her first few weeks, I watched as she struggled with parental communication, maintaining adequate lesson plans, and providing timely feedback to her students. She experimented with a variety of classroom management plans. She often stayed at work late into the evenings trying to make sense of her struggles, but nothing seemed to work. Then one day, late in November, she came to me with tears in her eyes, explaining that she had decided teaching just wasn't for her. It was a lot harder than she thought it would be, and perhaps it just wasn't her calling, even though she had spent the better part of the last decade dreaming of having her own classroom to help teach the next generation.

In some schools and districts today, this conversation would have led to the teacher's dismissal. Some administrators would have agreed with this young teacher, decided that changing her mind and changing her practice was too much effort and let her go. They would have found a substitute teacher or other newly certified teacher to fill in and start all over again. In some districts, every year there is a hunt for new teachers, as the experiment of finding new teachers who already have it all figured out, fails to meet the hoped-for results. The reality is that the only way for any of us to really learn how to teach is to teach. Lord knows that I am a way better educator today than I was twenty years ago, and I hope that the same can be said twenty years into the future. There is a reason veteran teachers in almost every school system in America make more money than their rookie peers. The belief is that once you have had time to refine your craft, to make mistakes, to learn and grow, you can have a more powerful impact. The first few years are going to be rocky. There are going to be some missteps, but it is the responsibility of a strong leader to help foster growth, to nourish confidence, and provide support for learning.

This same mindset is essential within classrooms as well. Our students come into our classrooms in need of guidance. They need our support, and they need our high-quality teaching. If they come to us with all of the answers, with all of the skills, and all of the attributes to be successful without us, then perhaps we are not needed. The truth is, every student needs a great teacher. Every student has the opportunity to grow beyond where they currently are. Every student will make mistakes, and every student will have some success. In our classrooms, we must collect evidence to not only document this but to also help us organize our plans as well. In a middle school or high school, it is not uncommon for a teacher to have 150 students per day. In an elementary school, a teacher may have 30 students assigned to her but may be asked to teach each student four or five different subjects. Being able to identify the core competencies, the strengths and struggles for each, being able to organize and plan to meet the unique needs of each student can be extremely overwhelming. In some systems, we have decided to take the easy approach, to assess kids early and often, and to write off those who come to us without the required skills before we have even had a chance to nurture them. In other systems, students are compared to a norm as all students are presented with the same material, in the same way, and those who can show they "get it" are rewarded with a good letter grade, high G.P.A., and Honor Roll sticker. At the same time, those who fall behind are given a low letter grade, may have a label placed upon them, and may be asked to repeat the grade all over again, or go get separate instruction from a different adult, often one with less skill and experience than the classroom teacher to whom they were assigned. This just doesn't make sense.

Just as a new teacher deserves the opportunity to be supported, to be coached, and to be developed, so do individual students within our schools. There are veteran teachers in our system who may not fully embrace technology, may not understand the evolving standards, and may need targeted training in emerging best practices. We do not simply write these teachers off. We focus on their unique needs and develop a plan to equip them for continued success. If this is good enough for teachers, it is good enough for our kids.

In our classrooms, we have to stop holding early struggles against a student who may eventually come to an understanding later on. (The teacher who I described earlier is now actually one of the most gifted teachers I have ever seen. I am so glad neither of us decided to actually give up.) In too many classrooms, we put more of an emphasis on WHEN a student gains understanding than we do on WHAT she understands. Should a teacher who struggled in her first year, be labeled as a deficient teacher in year five, even if she has found her way and is showing signs of success? Should a teacher who has a misstep in September, but eventually shows evidence of learning from her feedback and demonstrates through observations and reflections an ability to teach at a high level in May, have her two experiences averaged together for a less than stellar final evaluation score? I think not. Why in classrooms do we then take early struggles and use them against a student in both our grade books and our support processes if we do not think the same methodologies should apply to us? We need to quit being so MEAN.

In most of our schools today, student scores, student successes, student struggles are averaged together to create an aggregate based on the mean. The mean is that score you get when you add all of the scores earned together and divide by the total number of opportunities. For example, if a student has the following scores on tests in a class this marking period: 95, 75, 82, 45, 35, 40 he may end up with an average score of 62 simply because we take each of his six scores, add them together, and divide by 6, the total number of scores earned. What's interesting is that with this method of calculating a student's grades we would also assign a final grade of 62 to the student who earned the following scores: 62, 62, 62, 62, 62, 62 AND to the student who earned these scores: 10, 20, 50, 92, 100, 100.

Student A	95	75	82	45	35	40	MEAN 62
Student B	62	62	62	62	62	62	MEAN 62
Student C	10	20	50	92	100	100	MEAN 62

When we use the mean to create an aggregate average score, we are making quite a few assumptions, assumptions that quite frankly, most of us would admit are unintentional and not accurate.

The first assumption we make is that each of these six assessments that the students took measure the same thing and should carry the same weight. Perhaps this was the same test taken six times for some reason, and that each test was designed to measure student understanding of the same content. If that is the case, we have even more questions. Within the given test, are we to assume that every item measured student understanding of the same content, or are there multiple skills and understandings being measured within the assessment? Has the content advanced or progressed in depth? If it is the same content and skill, why would the same student be able to be successful with some of the assessment, but not all of it? Are all the questions created equally? If it is not the same skills and content being measured with each item on the assessment, when we see aggregate grades of 50, 82, or even 90, do we know what information the given students have mastered and what they haven't? When we use percentages as our strategy for giving graded feedback, do we know what we are implying?

Percentages really only work when measuring one thing, one standard, or one skill, and trying to determine the frequency, or how often, success is found, for example, how often a basketball player can make a free throw, or how often a place kicker can make a field goal. Even with the latter example, things can get tricky as sometimes the kicks take place indoors, and sometimes they are outdoors. Sometimes the kick happens from 20 yards away, sometimes it is 50 yards away. Sometimes a lineman lets the kick get blocked, and sometimes the wind starts blowing. The more variables there are, the less reasonable it is to use a percentage as a measure of success. On a classroom assessment, when there may be multiple questions relating to multiple content standards, describing success with a simple percentage reflecting the overall success rate, makes it very difficult to pinpoint where to make corrections.

Using the example from above describing the three students who each scored a 62% mean score (average), our class record book would also show a class average of 62% because each of our students finished with this average. As a teacher, I may look at that average and be concerned. In most schools, this grade is then translated another time to a letter grade of a D or D-. (Some schools may actually say these students all get a grade of C because they are all at the "average," but that is another conversation.) When we look at the scores earned by **each** student instead of the average of **every** student, we actually see three different stories showing a variety of levels of success.

To simplify things, let's assume each assessment measures the same skill or content and that each question on each assessment carries with it the same level of difficulty measuring that single skillset or content standard. Student A, the student with the following scores (95, 75, 82, 45, 35, 40), is a student who regressed during the six weeks. There was evidence of mastery very early on when he demonstrated a 95% success rate. Assuming these grades are based on traditional percentages, this student showed during the beginning of the unit that he was already able to earn a score very close to the upper limit of 100. As time goes by, however, this student's score begins to take a dip. There are a lot of possible factors. Perhaps this student lost motivation after showing early on how successful he could be, and now, after six weeks, he is completely disengaged. Perhaps this was a student who was able to demonstrate mastery and understanding using a method or process of his own choosing (think math class). As time has gone by, the teacher has introduced a different method that has now left the student more confused than he was early on. Maybe there was a tragic life event that occurred within his family. The possible explanations are endless, and unfortunately, just looking at a final score of 62 tells us very little. As a matter of fact, even looking at the individual assessment scores, we still have a lot of questions

Student B (62,62,62,62,62, 62) has a much different story. This student shows a level of consistency, unlike either of the other two students. When we look at her scores, we could assume the student has shown no growth, but again, there is so much we do not know. We do not know if this student continued to show mastery of the same skills and content each time or if her success fluctuated between items. Maybe in the first week, she missed questions 1 and 2, but the following week missed questions 3 and 4. Maybe each week, she showed a different level of understanding even though her final grade remained the same. We do not know if the student showed mastery on items that were low level or more complex. In some class-rooms, this student may have actually demonstrated mastery of all of the content, but continued to lose points because of compliance issues like not showing her work, not putting her name on the paper, or having sloppy handwriting.

Many would look at Student C (10, 20, 50, 92, 100, 100) and argue that this student is the true success story. This was a student who very early on showed very little understanding, but thanks to hard work and amazing teaching, within a few short weeks showed evidence of success that far surpassed those of the other students in the class. As a matter of fact, this student even earned perfect scores twice, yet when final grades were reported, she earned a 62, just like her peers.

As a student, or as a parent, we often use report card grades, parent portal scores, or progress reports to gauge the academic progress of our students. In this scenario, each of these students is being sent home at the end of six weeks with the same story to tell, although the events that led to their stories are quite different. When we report scores based on the mean, not only do we not tell a full story, we often tell a false narrative. We do not take into account growth. We do not take into account individual skills and content. We do not take into account potential progress or decline.

As the parent of student C, I should be ecstatic and celebrating amazing improvement, but based on the final grade, I am not sure that I would. As the parent of Student A, I should be questioning why my student was not being enriched or progressing to new content after early success. Still, instead, I am left questioning whether there was any understanding of the material at all. As educators, we have to be very careful when we use the mean. We use it for a variety of reasons. It is easy. It is what was done to us. It helps us sort and select students, etc...but often, because of these same factors, we are left without having any truly valuable information. We may be able to label students as a result of this, but we are rarely able to make any useful adjustments, provide specific feedback, or draw accurate conclusions, and that is just MEAN. If you stick with this book all the way through Chapter Six, I am confident you will learn what to do instead.

* * *

GROWING UP AS A CHILD, I WOULD WAKE UP EARLY ON SATURDAY mornings to be able to get my weekly fix of cartoons on TV. We didn't have channels dedicated to twenty-four hours a day children's programming or YouTube Kids like we do today, so getting up before the sun, and sneaking out to the living room without disturbing my parents was my weekly ritual to get access to my shows. I loved watching Looney Tunes and seeing the shenanigans each of the animated characters was up to. As I watched my cartoons each week, I often saw a scene play out that many of you can probably remember as well. One of the characters would be caught in a tight spot. He may have been chased by a coyote or perhaps was let out of his bird cage with a cat in pursuit. As the character tried to determine how to generate a plan for survival, it finally hit him, and he had an idea. We would always know when the idea arrived because the illustrators would show us by inserting the image of a light bulb above the character's head as though his thoughts were now clearly illuminated.

Because of this simple illustration, many of us grew up believing that was how ideas, thoughts, and understanding came to fruition. We would be in the dark with no clear understanding, then poof, out of the blue, the idea would come to us, and a light bulb would come on. The reality is, however, that learning is not a binary, got it--don't got it, phenomenon. Learning is a process. It is more akin to stage lighting attached to an ever-increasing dimmer switch that slowly slides up, and sometimes down, as experiences provide us with new insights. In most of our classrooms, as we chase proficiency and grade-level expectations, we often make the mistake of oversimplifying what learning looks like and, as a result, miss the mark in both how we assess and how we instruct.

We must have a standard we use as our expectation. We must have a target. But, what we actually see is that with how most of us use our grading systems today, a student's journey towards meeting that target or becoming proficient actually has very little impact on what is reported on a final report card or even on any given assignment.

Let's say you do focus on standards-based instruction in your school. Let's assume that each day you have a learning target on the board that informs your classroom plans and that students are always actively engaged in activities that support the identified state adopted standard. If this really were your classroom, and maybe it is, what grade would you assign to describe a student who has shown mastery of the content standard? An A? 100%? What is the difference in understanding for a student who earns a B? What is the difference between a student who earns a 65% and a student who earns a 59%? You are teaching to a standard, but what do these scores show you and your students regarding their mastery of the standard? Do your grades reflect the percentage of times a student has shown mastery? A student who earns a 100% has shown perfection, whereas a student with an 80 has shown perfection eight out of ten times. Should your grades simply show that a student has shown mastery or hasn't, that they "got it" or "don't got it"? Should grades be a simple yes or no? How often should a student have to show mastery to prove they really understand your content? If they show they can perform a task once, are they done? Is five times enough? What if they show mastery in September, should they still be masters in May?

Let's bring out again the question of what is best for you as a teacher. As a certified and qualified teacher, how many times should you be observed by your supervisor during the school year to prove that you are a master teacher? If in September your supervisor visits your classroom, clipboard in hand, and you earn highly effective status on every indicator used to measure your competence, should your administrator come back each day for 180 days to make sure you are still displaying that high-quality evidence? If you struggle at the beginning of the year, but in May have figured it all out and are observed finally "getting it," what should your final evaluation score be? Should teachers' observation scores from multiple years, or even across several months, be averaged together? I think not. And I don't think we should be doing this with the grades of students either. When we take the easy out, the MEAN way out, we are discounting feedback, coaching, and the ability to grow and improve. If we shouldn't be using the average, or more specifically, if we should stop being MEAN, what should we be doing? Later in this book, we will go into more specific details, but for now, there are really three primary points of emphasis to get you started:

1. Determine what really matters
2. Determine the frequency in which you will measure for understanding
3. Agree that you will focus on what is most recent, not what is MEAN

Step 1: Determine what matters most.

A few years ago, I published a book titled *It's Like Riding a Bike: How to Make Learning Last a Lifetime* in which I go into a much more thorough explanation of this. Still, in essence, we as educators must determine the purpose behind every task we have our students do and every question we want them to answer. Too often, our grade books have become a collection of misaligned information, lacking the specificity needed to make informed decisions. We give our students worksheets and tests asking students multiple questions relating to a variety of topics, standards, and skills with no way for us to effectively determine what a student knows and what he is still struggling with by simply looking at a final score. If we have a learning target identified, we need to be sure we are assessing that target. When a basketball player is standing on the free-throw line, he is being measured based on his ability to put the ball through the hoop, not his ability to bounce the ball three times, how many rotations of backspin he can put on the ball, or whether he shoots in five seconds or nine seconds. He is being measured against one standard and one standard only. If it goes in, we celebrate. If he misses, we can then provide coaching and guidance on strategies to help with future attempts, but will then again measure his success with meeting the target.

Often in our classrooms, our grades go beyond reflecting a student's success in meeting a target, but they also often incorporate our opinion of whether the target was hit according to how we would do it, using the strategies we have introduced, the behaviors we think are important, instead of being a simple reflection of how close the students have come to meeting the standard. The first step is simple- determine what kids need to know and what it will look like when they do. The ambiguity comes into play when we attempt to measure if they do it your way or not.

Step 2: Determine the frequency in which you will measure for understanding.

How often should a student be expected to demonstrate that they still "got it," and how often do you let a student try to show you that they finally "get it?" The truth is there is no real science behind this. It is really a matter of comfort, planning, and prioritization. If you teach 150 students, the struggle can be intense to allow frequent retakes, reassessments, and new attempts. If you assign essay tests (more on this later) or projects to your students as your primary assessment method, allowing students to continue to refine and redo tasks can be a burden. (Of note the final version of this book underwent more than two dozen re-writes, just sayin'. Not to mention, your favorite album, movie, and TV show probably all went through hundreds of retakes and mixes, before being deemed ready for distribution as well).

To manage student retakes, in some classrooms, teachers have found success with assessment tickets where students must plead their case for a reassessment and demonstrate what they have done to earn this opportunity. In some classes, teachers provide one question re-takes that are all or nothing for a student to show future mastery. In some classes, teachers provide spiraled assessments (more in chapter 6). While in others, rubrics drive the grading. How often you allow students to show mastery is really a teacher decision or one that can be collectively determined with a teacher team, but there are two guiding principles:

- assessment should not be a one and done phenomenon.
- the evaluator of assessment should not average all attempts together.

We already discussed the pitfalls of averaging with a MEAN score, so let's address the logic behind a one and done. Beginner's luck, a fluke, chance, whatever you call it, you know what I am talking about. Remember the aim of grading, the aim of assessing is to express as accurately as possible internal thoughts via external measures. When we provide feedback to a recipient, whether through conversation, narrative prose, or a letter grade, we need to make sure the recipient is open and ready to receive it. They have to believe the feedback is a result of quality evidence and observation. When we provide final feedback as a result of one encounter or one assessment, our inferences may be 100% spot on and accurate, but maybe they are not. This doubt, this margin of error, is what we have to attempt to diminish with our reporting.

A running back who carries the ball one time and runs 99 yards for a touchdown has an amazing success rate. But if he is asked to carry the ball thirty times a game, odds are, he is not scoring thirty touchdowns. Although it may be easier to calculate feedback based on a singular moment in time, there is still a high level of doubt regarding the reliability of that evidence. Look at that. I just threw a statistical term out there, and you didn't even notice. Reliability is simply our ability to believe the results are accurate and would hold up consistently. When we only assess once, we greatly reduce our reliability in the results, as a matter of fact, one could argue there is no reliability as we have no ability to see consistency. When we tell someone we rely on them, it means we believe in them. We think they will come through for us. When we collect evidence of learning, we must be able to ask ourselves the same questions and walk away with a reasonable belief that results will be consistent. Just like trust in a person is rarely earned after a singular encounter, trust in evidence should carry the same burden. How long does it take to earn trust? It depends. How much evidence is enough to prove the reliability of a grade? It depends…. I know. That's a soft answer, but it's a real answer. Remember, trust takes a long time to earn, but a moment to lose. The same is true when we speak of assessment reliability. A one and done test may yield a false positive, but continued positive results, yield growing confidence in the results. A false positive inhibits our ability to offer needed support. The goal is to have confidence in the results we collect so that the decisions we make have meaning and value. The more confidence you have, the more willing you are to dismiss data outliers that send a different message and contradict every other piece of evidence you have.

Step 3: Agree that you will focus on what is most recent, not what is MEAN.

This has been covered already, but using past mistakes against someone who has shown current growth, just isn't fair or accurate. Some will argue that the preponderance of evidence is the way to go (this is sometimes referred to as the mode). They believe that instead of using the mean to determine the average, we should use the score that is most frequently earned, regardless of when it was earned. For example, if a student earns the following grades 62, 62, 65, 75, 89, 100, some would argue this student should earn a 62 because it is most frequently earned. I disagree.

The mode is a great way to look at holistic scores like class averages or frequency data (which items on an assignment do most kids struggle with, for example). Still, when working with individual students, our focus should always be on growth. We want to know what a student is capable of today and how much progress he has made, and we do this by eliminating as many arbitrary deadlines as possible. We can't tell every student that they must have mastery by Friday, because Friday is always test day, and not allow students to show future understanding if they finally "get it" over the weekend. If you fail your drivers' license test, struggle with your ACT, or fail your teacher certification exam, you can always retake it (sometimes for a cost), but your past struggles are never averaged with your current success. Only in schools do we use cumulative G.P.A.'s that put no weighting on recency and aggregate averages in a classroom with no focus on growth, to paint a picture of a person in a holistic, and often a completely inaccurate way. If a kid shows today that they can earn a grade higher than what they earned three weeks ago, change it. This just shows that you did an excellent job of teaching and inspiring hope. It is not an indictment of the kid. It is a celebration of your ability to teach.

I know the thought running through some of your heads, "But...my state only gives my students one chance to take a test and makes high stakes judgments and decisions based on the results." Yes, they do...and no, they don't. I promised you in the first pages of this book that I would avoid a lot of statistical mumbo jumbo, so let me try to walk a thin line. The first line of this chapter reads, "a test cannot be valid or invalid, but the inferences we draw from them can be." The short and sweet of it is that most state-level assessments are actually very good assessments. Our interpretation of what the assessments are measuring and what those measurements are actually telling us is what often leads to poor legislative decisions and misaligned school-based practices. Most state-level assessments are designed to inform us about the frequency in which individual students are able to demonstrate competencies on specifically designated standards. Some assessments provide specialized weighting by providing ques-tions that are perceived to measure standards of greater depth, of high order thinking, or greater cognitive complexity, more points than those perceived to be lower-level or of relatively less complexity. Scores earned then get added together to create a total scale score. Often we assume a student with a higher scale score knows more than a student with a lower scale score, but this is not always the case. A higher score can be earned often by knowing "less" but knowing "less" at a deeper level. A student may get more of the higher weighted items correct and get a higher score than a student who actually gets a greater frequency of questions correct. Think about it like the game Jeopardy. One contestant may get four $100 questions correct, and another contestant may get one $500 question correct. Contestant A has a scale score of $400, while contestant B has a scale score of $500. We can't determine who knows more with a score like this, and we certainly should not be setting cut scores to determine minimum levels of proficiency as a result of scores like this.

The test itself is actually doing a great job of measuring student mastery of content. It is probably varied and dynamic, providing multiple questions to assess single standards so as to not be "one and done." It is designed to assess skill progression by measuring varying degrees of understanding, yet, because we often do not understand what the test does or does not do, we begin making assumptions and destiny sealing decisions.

Let me also quickly state that no two tests are the same. Just as we need to recognize the unique nature of each student, we need to recognize the unique nature of each assessment. With this book, I am making some fairly generalized statements to try and create more universal understanding. I strongly encourage you, once you are armed with just enough knowledge to make your supervisor's life miserable, to dig into the test design you are currently asked to administer and ask a lot of questions to seek more understanding.

The next myth I want to debunk is that very few assessments administered summatively accurately reflect growth. Depending on where you live and work, growth can mean different things. Just as the word "data' has been distorted to now have a negative connotation in the minds of so many, growth, in its purest sense, is simply progress over time. Sure, we have legislation requiring growth-based assessments in almost every state in the U.S. Sure, we have assessments that market themselves by producing a growth score of some variety, but rarely, and by rarely I mean I am yet to find one that does, do they actually measure individual student progress in learning.

Let's go back to the analogy that was used earlier about a baseball player's batting average. My third child is six years old and loves to play baseball, and he's pretty good at it. In his league, he is one of the best. I say this because, against the other six-year-olds, he is crushing the ball, making amazing catches, and throwing the ball across the diamond when many others are still picking dandelions and kicking dirt. Actually, last season he had a batting average of .750, meaning he got a hit three out of every four times he went to the plate. Let's pretend that next year he gets elevated to play on a team with seven and eight-year-olds. On this new team, he is now facing pitchers who have had another year or two of experience and who are stronger and can throw faster. Next year my son has a batting average of .500; he now only gets a hit half of the time. Does this mean he has regressed in his ability to hit? Does this mean he has gone backward? No, not at all. It means he is facing different conditions and being asked to perform against different variables. The same is often true with state assessments.

State assessments are often built to measure student understanding of grade-level content. This means question items are designed so that if a third-grade reading standard asks students to analyze the development of a main character in a narrative text, there are questions asking students to analyze the main characters in a narrative text. In fourth grade, a standard might ask for students to be able to compare two main characters in a text, so guess what? The assessment should ask students to compare two main characters in a text. Although both standards center around character development, analyzing a single character and comparing multiple characters are different skills. Using a score on a third-grade assessment based on a third-grade standard and comparing that to a score on a fourth-grade assessment measuring a fourth-grade standard does not tell us if a child has shown growth. As the old saying goes, it's apples and oranges. Sure we can come up with a weighted scale score for third grade standards, and sure we can come up with a similar weighted score for fourth grade standards, but we cannot simply subtract the difference and call it growth. Again, simply looking at a weighted score, a scale score, doesn't tell us where proficiencies are or are not. They simply paint an overall picture. It's like taking your child to the doctor, and they measure his height at 48 inches and his weight at 72 lbs. Adding both together, you are told that your child has a total score of 120. The following year after the tests are performed again, and you are told your child now has a score of 150. We can assume this means healthy growth, but if the only number that has grown is his weight,

HEALTHY growth may not be the case. It would be even more confusing if, at eight years old, instead of measuring weight and height, your doctor began measuring body mass index and adding that to head circumference. Measuring something completely different makes a comparison that much harder, yet this is what we have been trained to do in schools, far too often, with some pretty drastic consequences.

Some states now have legislation requiring students to be retained, held back to repeat a year of school, if minimum benchmarks are not met or if "growth" is not observed. Many districts have policies in place whereby students receive special labels, labels that cannot be easily removed, identifying them as having disorders, as a result of errors in score interpretation. We must understand what our tests can and cannot do. They cannot make inferences. That is up to us.

4

DON'T LABEL THE BOX

When you tell teachers that they are judged only by how students score on a test, you will get teachers who cover a lot of content. When you tell teachers they are all judged by a student's desire to keep learning, you will get teachers who put their passions on display.

I loved being a school principal, especially a middle school principal. I've said it before, but it's worth saying again, middle school is not for everyone. If you are an adult and you don't absolutely love middle school kids, then do not sign up to work in a middle school, because those kids will eat you up and spit you out. It is such an awkward time for so many of them as they wrestle with hormones, body changes, social drama, and the increase in expectations coupled with a desire for new levels of independence. The teachers I worked with in my middle schools were all incredible. They understood their role involved more than just being the masters of the curriculum. Their job was to also help their students learn to be comfortable in their own skin.

One year I came up with the idea to do an activity to help reach each child in a way that required every staff member to step outside of their comfort zones and be a little vulnerable. I asked each staff member to bring in a picture of themself from middle school to display along with the following message, "It's not about who you were; it's who you are that determines who you will be." The activity helped create a lot of laughs, both from the staff and the students, as they walked the halls and saw pictures outside of every classroom and office space, of adults from the prime of their youth. The goal was bigger than just providing laughs, though. We hoped the activity would also provide a little bit of hope for the students' futures, beyond the awkward pre-teen years. While serving as a great bonding experience for the staff, the activity was also designed to show our students that all of us lived through the awkward stage, all of us grew out of it. For me, the activity also did something else. While I was flipping through one of my old photo albums, hoping to find the perfect picture of the thirteen-year-old version of Dave, sporting short shorts, knee-high socks, buck teeth, and feathered bangs, I stumbled upon a picture I had long ago forgotten about. It was an image of me as a twelve-year-old boy sitting in a large cardboard box.

I grew up as a Navy brat. Having a father who served in the military meant that my family was asked to relocate often. As a matter of fact, I attended sixteen different schools growing up. While my family and I were relocating, so were all of our household goods. I spent a great deal of my childhood packing and unpacking. The image displayed in this forgotten photograph I discovered showed a picture of me, soon after making one of our many moves. My family had just moved into a new house, and all of my toys and clothes had just been delivered. Looking back on it now, I remember that I had been asked to spend the previous month surviving with only the items that could fit into one suitcase. On the day this picture was taken, all of my other personal possessions had arrived, all of my toys, clothes, sports equipment, everything. When my parents came into my room and snapped this picture with what I assume was a recently unpacked Polaroid camera, I am sure they assumed I would be playing in a huge pile of toys. Instead, they found a pile of my toys sitting on the floor next to me and me seated inside a large box, with a hat on my head turned backward sporting a pair of 7-11 sunglasses. I had turned one of my packing boxes into a fighter jet, in my mind, and I was the pilot. I was flying across the ocean, shooting down the enemy, just like Tom Cruise had done in *Top Gun*. What the photograph did not show was that the next day, that same box was converted into a racecar, and the day after that, it was King Tut's tomb. That box sparked hours of creative fun. It wasn't what the designers of that box intended? It was designed to hold personal items for easy shipping. My parents had even taken a permanent marker to the side of it and labeled it Dave's Toys. But I had used my imagination to turn it into so much more.

The photograph I found illustrates what I believe is a great metaphor for what is and is not working in our schools today. In education today, we are constantly looking for the silver bullet to student engagement, student learning, student inquiry, and student assessment. We read articles, explore Twitter, and attend conferences in an attempt to hear the one-trick necessary to increase our bottom line (student achievement). Unfortunately, what we often do as a result of all of this learning is place ourselves in a box, slap a label on it, and lose our creativity. We think one initiative, one tool, one pre-packaged / pre-labeled program is going to be the answer. We try to find a script to follow; we forget we have kids to reach and get frustrated when we don't get the intended results.

For the past ten years, the terms formative and summative assessment have been used by countless "experts" to describe how we need to evaluate student learning. Often teachers learn about these two formats and try to craft two different types of assessments to fit their varied needs. We are told that teachers must create a formative assessment to evaluate teacher effectiveness. We are told teachers must create summative assessments to evaluate student learning. We place these assessments into two separate boxes, label them, and use them only for their pre-planned purposes.

Don't get me wrong. Using formative and summative assessments are crucial components of high-quality teaching. At my own schools, we have spent our time talking about little else, but what we lose sight of is the fact that the best assessments are not formative OR summative, but instead serve both purposes, not one exclusively. Placing a label on an assessment before using the assessment is unnecessarily restricting. Teachers should be able to give an assessment and use it formatively and summatively. The label on the assessment should not be applied until after it has been used. Placing it on prematurely places us in a labeled box.

If we label a task as summative and we do not get the intended results indicating student learning, does this mean a teacher should not adjust his or her instruction? A summative assessment should not just be used as a capstone or ending point in learning if we have reason to believe there is still room for more learning to occur. Similarly, if we label that same task as formative, but every kid shows mastery of the skill, are we not supposed to claim this as evidence of proficiency or do we just consider it "practice" and require a student to show the same level of mastery later on a task we have arbitrarily decided to count as more valuable? A great assessment allows us to use it formatively to evaluate our own instruction AND summatively by assessing student understanding. It is how the task is used, not how it is designed, that yields results.

Assessment is critical. Teachers must be diligent to determine the validity and reliability of each assessment given, but this does not mean we must limit ourselves to the labels. When working on classroom instruction, teachers must not fool themselves into thinking there is only one way for a child to learn. There are countless ways for students to learn, just as there are countless ways for students to show what they have learned. We need to avoid putting our students into boxes that are already labeled. We need to avoid telling students there is only one way to do anything. We need to know how the story of our classroom will unfold, even though we may not necessarily know the themes that will emerge.

Great authors understand this. Titles of books are not written before the story is complete. Authors wait until they have developed an entire plot, then look for a way to synthesize the message. Singers do not determine which songs will be singles or the titles of their albums until the entire record has been crafted. As teachers, we need to learn to take our labels off and just go.

I do this at home with my own kids as often as possible as well. My oldest son likes to play with Legos. He has countless sets. He has bricks of every shape and color. When his sets are purchased, they always come in a box with directions. He used to follow the directions, assemble the pieces just right, and then…nothing. Once he had followed the manufacturer's directions, he saw his job as complete. He was not asked to be creative, inventive, or investigative. He simply followed the script. Now when I buy his Legos, the first thing I do is open the package and toss the directions into the garbage. Then I throw the new pieces into a bin with the rest of his Lego sets, and say "Have fun," leaving it up to him to learn, create, and "think outside of the box."

The kids we are teaching today will be asked to demonstrate that they understand the world in a way that is much different than we ever had to. Sure they will need to be able to follow directions, but more than that, they will be asked to write directions. They will be asked to identify problems and create solutions. They will all be asked to serve as an engineer in some capacity even though this may not be their career designation. They will be asked to design solutions, experiment, troubleshoot, and fail repeatedly. In our classrooms, we must get into the habit of having our students upload more than they download.

As teachers, don't put yourself, or your students, in a labeled box. And don't do this with any of your assignments or assessments (if you still consider these two different things). Of course, you need to stay organized, but the only time a box needs a label on it is when items are being moved from one place to another. Once it has arrived, scrub the labels off and let the creativity begin. Don't force your students to learn the way you learn. Let them learn how to learn. Don't force them to be assessed using one template. Let them demonstrate understanding by being creative. Help them identify the problems, but let them generate the solutions. Don't stick to the script when an adlib is necessary. Don't tell your students to climb out of the box because it was designed for something else. If your students climb in, help them create something that has value.

I am so lucky that on that day, thirty-some years ago, my parents let my toys sit on my bedroom floor and captured a picture of me playing in an empty box, a box that allowed my creative energies to be utilized, a box that was designed for one purpose, but was repurposed into something that has lasted a lifetime, a creative mind rooted in imagination. That box is a great memory. Had it only been used to pack up some old GI Joes, it would have been recycled and forgotten about. Because the label was removed, it instead has become a lasting memory. A memory that has changed the way I parent, the way I teach, the way I lead, and the way I assess.

Assessment has become synonymous with the word "test" in many schools. For some reason, throughout the history of the K-16 educational model in the U.S., many of us have come to believe that the only way to accurately measure student aptitude and ability is through a formal, high stakes, quiz, test, or exam. Yet, at the same time, this is also one of our biggest frustrations. Sure, many of us give assignments to our students during the week. We may even ask students to complete homework. Perhaps we give our students points for participation in class, but we have also come to believe that what matters most is how a student can do on a test. You may not think this, but the actions of so many of us demonstrate otherwise. Those other tasks and assignments have simply become hoops to jump through, as opposed to quality learning opportunities and evidence of learning, on the way to really demonstrating understanding in something we have treated as more valuable, in our weighting, in our grading, and even just in our terminology.

Because we understand that equity and equality are not the same things, in our schools, students with disabilities have accommodations written into their formalized Individualized Education Plans (IEP) indicating that their tests should be read aloud, that items should be reduced, or small group settings may be required. We have local districts asking teachers to weight their grade books so that tests have a larger impact on an overall score. Many secondary schools have policies mandating exams at the end of semesters that account for up to half of a final report card grade. I am not arguing against the effectiveness of tests, or the need for accommodations and modifications, as a matter of fact. I am not even arguing that standardized state assessments are a bad idea. What I am arguing is that how we use these (ahem...don't use these) is an issue.

We have to get ourselves to a place where we believe all assessment matters and can and should be used to both measure student understanding and to help us adjust our instructional practices.

We have trained teachers to believe that there are some assignments and tasks that we should assign to students simply for our benefit. We tell teachers that these tasks should not be graded or scored, and instead of that, we, the educators, should use them to determine our next steps. We say these are just "practice" or "formative." We then use our own subjective opinions to create another assignment or task that we decide to score and grade. We call it "summative," then use those grades to label and identify students. So, in essence, we commit to making instructional decisions and adjustments using data that we claim isn't as reliable or valuable, then give students a task that we determine to be more valid and of higher quality and do nothing with those results.

If you are a teacher, let me ask you, how do you determine when to give a test? If you know your students are ready, why do you need to give it? If you are not sure if your students are ready, why are you giving it? If you are assigning tasks to students that you believe will help inform your teaching, you are making a claim that the inferences you acquire as a result have value. If a student is able to demonstrate through an assignment that you previously designated as 'formative," that he or she has an understanding of the content, then it is your responsibility to document that evidence. Likewise, if a student struggles on a task that you previously labeled as summative, it is your responsibility to provide alternate instructions and to make informed, professional decisions on the next steps. Evidence is evidence. We cannot blame our systems, our districts, or our schools for the grading policies in place. We are the systems. We are the districts and schools. We have to be willing to ask the questions and have the conversations that change the practices, policies, and mandates.

When a lawyer presents his case to a jury, he does not describe some evidence as quality evidence and some as circumstantial. Circumstantial evidence is not reliable and is thrown out. Some evidence is relevant, and some is not, but once it is admissible, it all helps shape the verdict. In our classrooms, for us to really begin to analyze data, and to begin to make informed decisions that can benefit the students we love, we must begin to examine the evidence as if it all tells part of the story. The task you gave to your students to work on Tuesday evening is just as much a part of the story as the final exam they took last June. If we are giving our students tasks to complete that do not offer information to us as educators helping us determine what our next steps should be, then we need to scrap the tasks and start over.

In Chapter One, I described the confusion we create when we provide multiple translations of the same story, whether in text or in grading. I explained that with assessment, we convert internal knowledge into external outcomes. Then we convert external outcomes into quantifiable scores. Then we convert those scores into letter grades that we send home to parents and expect them to make meaning of. But the reality is if our grades said it all, if they accurately reported what each student understood and didn't understand, we would not need parent-teacher conferences. The truth of the matter is that so many parent-teacher conferences that I have attended as a parent, a teacher, and an administrator have been spent listening to someone explain grades and scores because what we sent home previously did not accurately tell the whole story. I have heard countless teachers make the claim to parents and students that if their child would just "work harder" or "study more," his or her grade would improve. This is a statement which honestly makes me really question if the grade assigned was ever really a representation of knowledge, or if it was more accurately a description of work habits.

I am not quite sure how a thirteen-year-old tries harder to learn something. I honestly do not know what that looks like. I know it may represent more effort in completing tasks or maybe spending more time reading a book, but knowledge is not something you acquire by working hard until you "got it." It is gained through a process.

To add to the confusion of knowledge translation, let me introduce scale scores, proficiency bands, percentile rankings, DRA levels, reading levels, and RIT points. It's like we realized the matrix we were using with our class grade scales was not confusing enough, so instead of simply cleaning those up, we decided to complicate things even more. We have so many different reports to pull from, so many different data points, that instead of using a variety of assessments to verify our results, we decide to treat some assessments as though they are faulty, don't tell us much, don't align with what we already know, or we dismiss them altogether.

There are so many districts, and entire states now, that mandate that students be assessed in a standardized format multiple times a year. In theory, this assessment protocol is designed to inform teachers on how to intervene on behalf of their students, but this is often perverted and used instead as a prediction of success on state accountability tests. I am going to be very direct when I say this. Using one assessment to predict success on a future assessment is educational malpractice. Doing so simply perpetuates stagnation and implies a lack of hope. We are indicating that quality instruction will not impact future success. We are labeling students based on past exposure to content without any indication of how future content will be understood. We begin to paint students as either "good" or "bad" based on aggregate understandings without taking into account future experiences and unassessed skill sets.

If you are assessing students just to determine which kids should be the center of attention, which students are on the "bubble" and require the most support, you have already fallen for the assessment trap. Remember, EACH kid matters. Knowing the difference between each and every is the difference. We cannot use student assessment as a means to just focus on getting every student to proficient. Each student has a different starting place and, therefore, should have a different ending place. Our job as educators is not to compare students to other students, but to compare students to themselves as they grow and develop. Each student has his own growth chart, and it is up to us to help them continue to develop. We have no idea when a child will reach his maximum height, but it is not up to us to tell students that they all need to stop growing when they reach the average. If I believed every man on earth should grow to be my height, 5'10," and I put procedures in place to stop feeding them once they arrived at that height, or made them wear stilts if they were not there yet, I would be seen as narcissistic and crazy. It would be crazy to assume every man would end up just like me. Yet this is what we often do to kids in our classroom.

• Last paragraph - powerful!

TALK ALL YOU WANT—ACTION MATTERS MORE

Evidence is really an argument to demonstrate competency—the best assessments allow for interpretation, decision, and action.

As teachers, we are asked to make thousands of decisions a day. Do we turn the lights on or off? Do we use a Power-Point presentation, or do we lecture from memorized notes? Do we have students complete the odd problems or the even? Do we call on Johnny or Susie? When I began my career in the late 1990s, it was popular to describe teaching as both an art and a science. The science was the research-based "best practice," and the art was the instructional decisions teachers made at the moment to respond to their students. I would argue that this is also true for assessment. It is both an art and a science. It is often a collection of quantifiable facts that require subjective (artistic) decision making. Just as an artist must utilize her knowledge of color, texture, shape, and patterns, to create a unique product, teachers must likewise understand basic elements of the science of teaching to allow for more substantial artistic decision making.

We must understand that every decision we make, even those that seem mundane and arbitrary, are always based on our inherent analysis of the environment. The purpose of assessment is not just to quantify knowledge, but to also help us make reasoned decisions regarding everything within our control. It's like getting dressed in the morning. You may first check the weather. You may look at your schedule for the day. Then you decide whether you are going with pants or a skirt, slacks, or shorts, a sweater, or a button-down. You pick out what you think is a good combo, then you look in the mirror to see if the reality is as good as your beliefs, then you head to the living room and ask a family member for their opinion on what you picked out. This is how data analysis and assessment should work. We use scientific observations to make artistic decisions. We then evaluate our decisions and inferences while also seeking the interpretations and inferences of others to either corroborate our beliefs or to refute them.

This is what is meant by reliability. Reliability is simply the degree to which other people's inferences match ours. Do you like the clothes you are wearing today? Do others? Great-- That means there is a high degree of reliability. When we grow to rely on people, we know we can depend on them. When our inferences about our assessments are reliable, we know we can depend on them. In our classrooms and schools, literally, every decision we make is based on scientific reasoning and subjective reactions. When you disagree with the suggestions or feedback given to you by an administrator after an observation, it is not necessarily a result of either of you being incorrect. It is just that the evidence collected and used carries with it a low degree of reliability.

When we turn all of the lights on in the room, are students more engaged? How do we know? When we use a PowerPoint, do students have greater comprehension? How do we know? If we call on Johnny, will his answer most accurately reflect the level of understanding of all students in the class? How do we know? Sometimes as teachers, we resort to our gut instincts to help us make our decisions, but the reality is, our gut instincts are not arbitrary. Your gut is simply a reflection of your bias. Your bias is a result of your past. Your past may or may not be reflected in your present. To help us make decisions that are in the best interests of the students we currently teach, we must learn to assess their needs. We cannot always rely on what we discovered in the past. Science requires us to look back and analyze our discoveries. Art requires us to use that knowledge to create novelty today. This is why assessment matters. When we simply rely on the science of teaching, we create the status quo. This is what causes us to keep doing what has always been done.

When we simply encourage innovation, we create a pendulum that swings wildly as each of us follows our own whims. When we learn to evaluate our results and analyze our successes and struggles, we can move forward and create learning that impacts the students we have today in the way they need it most. Soon you will have the chance to read about practical assessment strategies to measure student understanding and mastery. Still, before we discuss assessing students, we must first discuss how we assess ourselves. Tomorrow, ask yourself, "Was today a good day or a bad day, and how do I know?" At the end of each day, put yourself in a position to reflect on what happened, to measure successes and struggles, and to seek evidence to confirm your feelings. This basic level of self assessment is critical in moving forward, in growing, and in planning for progress.

As a former building administrator, I have had the opportunity to conduct hundreds of classroom observations. I have gone into some classrooms that I would subjectively describe as amazing, and I have been in some classrooms that I would subjectively describe as a disaster. The cool thing is, my opinion really doesn't matter. Often, my opinion is based on what I would do. As an administrator, I rarely know the students in any classroom as well as a teacher does. My opinions are often based on my own interests, my own passions, my own history, and my own experiences. What really matters more than any of that is what the students need in the classroom being observed, not what the students needed in my own classroom years ago. This same logic is true in any teacher's classroom today. Subjectively a teacher may believe that what she is doing in her classroom today is a great lesson because it worked in the past with a different group of students, but what matters more is what the students in the classroom today need. Sometimes the needs are the same. Sometimes they are different. Assessment helps you decide. Assessment, when done right, helps us eliminate our own subjective bias so we can make objective decisions. When I come down the stairs at home wearing my favorite Hawaiian shirt, cargo shorts, and flip flops, my subjective bias tells me I am comfortable and look just fine. The looks on the faces of my kids and the direct disagreement from my wife lets me know that my own personal opinion may not be as accurate or reflective to reality as I had hoped.

I heard another example recently when I was thinking about selling one of my houses. Because I have a goal of making a profit from my home and because I have an emotional attachment to my house and the memories connected to it, my opinion of the actual value of my house may not be an accurate reflection of what the market would determine. I have a seller's bias. I believe my house is worth more than it probably is simply because it's mine, because I want it to be worth more, and because I am emotionally invested in it. This same reality can sometimes appear in our classrooms as well where we are hoping for academic success, have an emotional attachment to our students, and may very well assume our perspective matches reality, when that may not always be the case.

Today, I've got a pretty sweet job title. During the day, I am the Executive Director of Curriculum and Instruction. It's a fancy title, but what does it really mean? I didn't create my title, and to be honest, I am not a huge fan of it. If I had the opportunity to change it, I would prefer to be known as the Chief Cheerleader of Teaching, but I don't have that luxury, so instead, the placard on my wall is five lines long, and it still doesn't really describe what I do each day. The label I have been given does not really describe the work I do, and truth be told, many people I work with, even those just down the hall, don't really know what I do. I spend some time writing grants. I spend some time analyzing numbers. I spend some time responding to e-mails and phone calls. I spend some time meeting with vendors, but most of the time, I am in classrooms observing, discussing, and debating quality instruction.

My label, like most labels assigned to people, doesn't really tell the full story. I do not have a detailed job description filed away in Human Resources, so I have had to try to figure it out for myself. I have had numerous conversations with people I work with about what my job entails. I've asked them to define for me the words of my title. We will discuss the first two words, "EXECUTIVE DIREC-TOR" later in the book, but the word CURRICULUM is another major component of my job title. Some have told me that they believe curriculum is a collection of instructional resources, the books and supplies teachers are given. Some have told me it is a collection of the standards identified by the state. Some have told me it is the hidden agenda behind all that we do. But my favorite definition of curriculum I have heard is, *The What that drives our How*. I love that!

In my job, I spend a lot of time helping teachers embrace their innovative passions by developing engaging lessons. I help support their quest for supporting resources and technologies, but all of this is for nothing if we cannot first identify WHY we do what we do. We must first identify the goal, the *What*, before we spend our time developing an amazing How. We must balance the art of teaching with the science of it.

When I was a classroom teacher, each year, I had the opportunity to teach at least a few sections of US History to 8th graders. I loved that class. During the year, I would spend months with my students discussing and debating the Bill of Rights. We would discuss legislative intent, judicial interpretation, and the evolution of societal norms. I would totally geek out on it. I would have amazing lessons that engaged and inspired my students, but as a result, by the time June rolled around, each year, I was left to plow through my instruction on the Civil War and Reconstruction.

Conversely, on the other end of the school, the other 8th grade US History teacher in the building absolutely loved teaching about The War Between the States. He would captivate his students in lessons about battles, strategy, and negotiation. It was his passion. As a result, however, his students missed out on the depth of learning surrounding the establishment of the Constitution.

I have no problem saying, students in both of our classes learned a ton. They all had great experiences, were engaged in lessons that pushed their thinking, and helped them grow, but it is also safe to say that at the end of the year, students from our classes left with much different foundations of knowledge. To some degree, that is OK; however, our ninth-grade peers who received our students the following year often had a difficult time moving forward as students came to them with vastly different understandings and knowledge bases.

Here in the state of Michigan, where I work, we have adopted our own version of The Common Core Standards and Next Generation Science Standards. I've said it before, but I'll say it again... a standard is only standard if it's standard. The reason Michigan, like every other state, has adopted standards is to try and create consistency in learning goals. The hope is that teachers within buildings, across districts, and around the state will all be able to more easily identify what is essential without drifting towards their own biases and interests, like what I did when I was in the classroom. The goal has been to eliminate the need for teachers from 3rd through 10th grade to feel the need to teach the definition of a main idea, to eliminate the need for every elementary teacher to have a unit on dinosaurs and volca-noes, and to help each teacher better understand the needs for both their students today, as well as how to establish a foundation for the future. On the surface, this makes a lot of sense; however, there are still a few problems.

Here in Michigan, there are 257 standards identified for a sixth-grade student. That number may not be an exact match to your current location, but I can say confidently that it is pretty close. Since the days of NCLB and now ESSA, here in the U.S., each state has adopted very similar standards and expectations, with often only minor adjust-ments due to political realities. These standards come from the subject areas of English Language Arts, Mathematics, Social Studies, and Science (The Core 4). Assuming there are no school closure days, there are 180 school days in a given school year. This means that students are expected to master a standard, every .7 days. (Keep in mind, again, a standard is only standard if it is standard). This means we have a base expectation for ALL students to reach. This is not an expectation to simply cover content, but for students to learn content. Because, here in Michigan, we also believe in the value of well-rounded students, when we include the "elective" courses of Art, Choir, and PE (the three most popular courses), our number of stan-dards for a sixth-grade student leaps to 1431. That is the equivalent of mastering a new standard every .125 days, or every hour of every day. Don't worry, we will discuss the definition of mastery later in the book, but until then, just thinking about mastery as "having under-standing" will suffice.

Getting all students to the point of mastery for 257 standards in a single school year is a monumental task. Teachers know how daunting this task is. Administrators know how improbable this task is. It seems everyone knows how difficult the task is, but rarely have our solutions to the problem helped. We have developed pacing guides (ahemmm, mandates) that require teachers to all be in the same place at the same time, regardless of student understanding. We have preached the word "fidelity," requiring teachers to all cover material and utilize resources in the same way at the same time to fit everything in. It is no shock, to me, that despite these efforts, student achievement results have shown no change in the last twenty years, in my home state, and I am sure, whatever state you are in, as well. But that is not to say, success is not possible. As a matter of fact, I have been lucky enough to witness firsthand what beating the projections and predictions is all about.

I have had a great career. I have worked in multiple districts, in multiple states, having multiple roles. I have been blessed to work in a few schools and districts that have defied state and national trends by actually showing dramatic improvements in student mastery. From 2011-2015, I led a school that jumped over 799 other schools in state Top to Bottom rankings. From 2015-2018, I served in a school, in a different state, with many of the same struggles, that was able to double its student learning gains. In my current district, we also showed double-digit gains last year. I would love to sit back and say this is all because of me. In the past, I may have actually done just that, but I know the truth. All of this success has nothing to do with me. It has everything to do with the teachers and their ability to focus on the focus. When teachers can identify WHAT really matters, the HOW becomes that much more meaningful.

As a leader, what I try to do is re-purpose the box teachers live in. In a lot of places, teachers are told when to teach, when to turn the page, and when to give the test. I have yet to see a school where this model has actually resulted in long term, sustainable positive results. Instead, I try to remind teachers that it is up to them to decide what gets taught when; however, I also work to remind them that they are not given the freedom to randomly dream up anything to be taught simply because it is of interest to them. They must choose from the menu presented to them by the state department of education. We use our list of standards like a dinner menu and collectively work to determine what has the most nutritional value for our students. We don't decide by only picking those items we enjoy and are palatable to our tastes. We decide based on what we determine to be the most substantive.

THE TOP 10 LIST—WHAT THE WHAT?

We begin by looking at the verbs within each standard. Every standard in every state has a verb derived from Bloom's Taxonomy (or Webb's Depth of Knowledge). This verb does not just discuss the content to be learned, but the skill to be acquired. For example, "main idea" may indeed be taught every year from 3rd-10th grade in language arts classrooms, as the content, but each year the verb in the standard changes, requiring greater depth and cognitive demand as students move through the system. Students may begin by learning the definition of a main idea, but by the time they are in high school, they may be synthesizing the main ideas from multiple texts to determine a central theme.

Each year, teachers examine the full list of standards and begin to make instructional decisions about what is needed most for their current batch of students. Remember that full list of 257 standards required to be taught in sixth grade, 114 of them are in English Language Arts alone. Just as teachers have the power to determine if they teach with the lights on or off on any given day, they also have the power to decide what gets taught on any given day. How do they decide? It's not arbitrary. It is a subjective evaluation of objective evidence. It is a balance of art and science.

Each year, teachers are asked to read the standards assigned to their subject area and grade level and then weight them according to Bloom's Taxonomy. Remember Bloom's Taxonomy, the most talked-about research in education that nobody has actually read? According to Benjamin Bloom's team of researchers, all learning fits somewhere within a taxonomy. Those items that are reserved for short-term memory are considered low-level tasks. In contrast, those which are more focused on long-term retention (the ultimate goal of school-based education) are considered more cognitively complex and high order tasks. As teachers read each standard, they work to identify the verb in each standard and identify the level of complexity for each. They then assign a numerical value to each standard based upon its level on Bloom's. For a full recap of Bloom's Taxonomy, check out *Taxonomy of educational objectives: The classification of educational goals (1956).*

Recall-1

Understanding-2

Application-3

Analysis-4

Synthesis-5

Evaluation-6

Creation-7

Benjamin Bloom's work has been debated by researchers since its inception; however, using the belief being that the standards that require more cognitive demands (greater depth) have greater value, is exactly what psychometricians and test architects in every state use as their framework. The standards rooted in high order skills are expected to have greater endurance in the minds of our students and the most transference to life outside of school. When we focus on recall skills, students cram for a test, then as soon as the test is over, purge their short-term memory to create space for new information. Items with greater depth get lodged into long-term memory, however.

Once teachers have read the standards and have weighted them according to depth, they then read the standards a second time, this time looking for standards they believe have leverage. In this case, we define leverage as items that provide value to other subject areas. Perhaps it is a reading standard that will also provide value to science or social studies. Perhaps it is a math standard asking students to create proofs that will allow for greater clarity in understanding how to analyze a text. Every standard that is believed to have leverage gets a bonus point added to its total.

Lastly, teachers are asked to identify the standards that have endurance, during a third reading of the list. If there are standards that will serve as prerequisites towards future understanding in subsequent years, again, a bonus point is added.

What I have discovered is that in every state, in every subject area, once these point totals are added up, we can easily create a top 10 list. I have done this same activity, not just with the teachers who work with me daily, but with teachers in schools across the country. Once we create point totals based on our subjective analysis of leverage and endurance, coupled with an objective analysis of depth, we are able to determine which standards have the most value and should become the focus of all that we do. We have had a few instances where we have expanded our list to twelve standards, but even that is a much more attainable goal than where we started off. These essential standards, our power standards, become our curriculum. Ten Power Standards become the driving force for all assessment during our 10-month school year. That is a lot easier to focus on than 257 standards over a 180 day school year.

As a result of the reduced list of standards, teachers can focus in for a month at a time on each standard to make sure students truly master content. These standards become the focus of assessment as they look to determine fidelity in learning. Giving teachers the ability to focus for a month at a time, instead of quickly plowing ahead at a predetermined pace, allows their creative energies to really be devoted to HOW they want to deliver content as opposed to feeling the pressure to race to the next big idea. Teachers are encouraged to cover everything, to introduce and expose students to all required content standards, but to FOCUS on the FOCUS.

When we establish our WHAT, it is a lot easier to measure our HOW. When we reach an understanding of what students must learn, it is easier to compare success across classrooms, among students, and between teachers to determine what works and what doesn't. When we are just plowing ahead, teaching a multitude of skills and content each day, assessing student understanding becomes a muddled mess resulting in a facade of strategies used to often trick our guts into believing we are on the right path. Asking students to give a thumbs up at the end of class if they "understand" or calling on Johnny to have him prove that the entire class has mastered a skill is often what causes a teacher to falsely believe it is OK to move ahead with the curriculum when in reality, as end of year exams often show, only about 50% of students truly had a thorough understanding of what mattered most. Formative assessments are not informal assessments. Formative assessments guide our next steps. If we do not have accurate data, asking informal questions that provide an inaccurate perception of reality may actually be more harmful than not asking any questions at all.

Again, assessments are not valid or invalid; only our inferences are. If we have assessment results that indicate that less than half of our students have mastered the curriculum, we really have three choices to make. We can dismiss the results as faulty and claim the test as misaligned. We can accept the results as accurate but ignore the requirement to take action because it is more convenient to continue on the established path, or we can accept the results as a call to action. I prefer the latter. I prefer to look at the results, determine their meaning, then make a plan for correction. So when we say we have a 50% average for student mastery, what do we really mean?

I hate it when people are MEAN. Not grumpy, irritable, or rude (although this is all bothersome too). I don't like it when people are MEAN, as in the average, or told they are normal or that they perform at a level just like everyone else. In statistics, the average is typically calculated one of three ways: using the mode (or the most frequent), the median (the middle), or the mean (the sum divided by the quantity). In most schools, we sort and select kids by use of the mean. We determine grades by the mean. We determine who is "advanced" and who is "at-risk" by looking at the mean, and to be quite frank, this is MEAN.

Let me use a few examples to illustrate why the mean does not work in schools, even though it is used almost everywhere (don't ever assume that just because something is popular that it equates to being right-- Bell bottoms were extremely popular a generation ago, after all).

Remember our three students from Chapter 3 that each ended up with a 62% average at the end of the marking period? Imagine that those three students are a set of triplets in your class. The kids look identical but are each extremely unique. It is up to us to find ways to assess each child so that we can adjust and adapt to their individual needs. When our assessments are focused, our focus can be on each student.

You see, when we use the MEAN, we are being cruel because we do not have answers to what really matters. It's like drawing a conclusion about a person by only looking at how they dress or how they talk. It's judging a book by its cover. When we use the MEAN, we can easily calculate a quantifiable final score, but it's a score that doesn't tell us much. It's a score that brings about more questions than answers.

So what do we do differently? I am so glad you asked...

We can start by looking for patterns of evidence, revolving around the belief that learning is a process, not a "got it," "don't got it" phenomenon, and that it ends by never ending. We can begin using every assessment as an opportunity to grow and learn. In Chapter 6, we will describe a few simple approaches to get you started, but first, let me address one more critical idea that I feel needs to be understood.

Using an assessment to predict a future assessment is not only a waste of time, but it is also malpractice!

How often have you heard people predict the future of a student because of his/her demographic information? How often have schools been designated winners or losers because of an algorithm? How often are teachers asked to give a student a test so that a computer can simply predict success on a future test? How many "experts" come to schools before the school year even starts to describe what they see as the needs.

In my job, I have the opportunity to work with teachers and administrators from all around the country. One of the most common complaints I hear from both groups is, "We test our kids too much!". That is an interesting statement., and I actually completely DISAGREE. I actually believe that we do not test our students enough. One of the reasons we have so many high stakes tests in schools today is because people, often bureaucrats working in state capital buildings, believe that we need an honest and accurate assessment of what our students can and cannot do. This sounds reasonable enough. The issue is that often in classrooms, how, when, and what we assess does not match up with these so-called "high stakes tests" requested by "experts," so we feel a disconnect and tension. As a result, those same bureaucrats come back into our schools, through legislative action, and ask for us to administer more tests so that we can get earlier and more frequent progress updates, or in some places, predictors of future success. In other words, **we ask students to simply take tests to predict their success on future tests.** There are some assessments available that actually use their ability to correlate and predict future performance as a selling point.

As I write this, we are in the heart of football season, one of the best times of the year. Just a few weeks ago, as summer was drawing to a close, pundits and "experts" from all across the country began making their predictions on what the upcoming seasons had in store.

I live in the middle of the mitten, known to many others as mid-Michigan. Where I live, the majority of people have loyalties to three football teams, the Michigan State Spartans, The University of Michigan Wolverines, and the Detroit Lions. Back on July 15th, prior to any games being played, the Spartans were not ranked by the "experts" to be in the Top 25 teams. The Wolverines were picked by "experts" to be possible national title contenders, and the Detroit Lions were predicted, by computer simulations, to start their season 0-10.

Well, a month into football season, it is safe to say we now know why they play the games. The Wolverines are a mess, the Spartans are up and down every week, and the Lions are actually being considered as one of the best teams in the NFL. I am so glad the experts, and the computers, don't have the power to actually label and define the winners and losers before the season ever starts. I mean, that would be crazy, wouldn't it? To simply look at the rosters of the teams, to enter that data into a computer, and then let the computer decide who the winners and losers are... enter assessments in most K-12 schools today.

In schools everywhere we have been conducting, what I believe to be, educational malpractice. We have decided to label kids, label schools, and label districts as a result of a computer algorithm. We have taken quantifiable data, entered it into a computer, a computer programmed by humans so that we can then predict future success or failure, and we don't give it a second thought. We do not question the reliability of these predictions. We do not ask for evidence that these simulations will reflect actual long-term results. We take it at face value that a student identified as "not proficient" will be "not successful."

Let's take this approach and connect it back to the football metaphor used earlier. Jim Harbaugh is the coach for the University of Michigan football team. If he bought into the hype this summer regarding his team's anticipated success (some may say he actually did) and he simply leaned into this prediction without making his own assessments of strength or weakness, without creating weekly game plans, without structuring practices to reduce weaknesses and highlight successes, would they ever be able to live up to the prediction? No way. On the flip side, what if the Detroit Lions bought into the belief that they would be winless for the first two months of the season. What would be the point of showing up to practice every day?

In our classrooms, we have unfortunately taken this same approach on a smaller level. We have begun classifying assessments as either formative or summative, often using formative as predictive assessments and summative as the assessments that "really matter." We may use weekly quizzes, computer-adaptive assessments, or department created assessments as a means to simply predict later success. In our grade books, we rationalize this by counting these "formative assessments" as a smaller weight while the summative carry the larger burden. But again, this is far from being pedagogically sound. If we truly love our students, we must begin to understand how assessments and the data they produce can help us move our students forward.

EVERY ASSESSMENT IS BOTH FORMATIVE AND SUMMATIVE

Formative assessment, by its very name, suggests that it should inform future action. A formative assessment is similar to a score at the end of the 1st quarter. It is an observation made by a coach at practice that his linemen are not getting low enough before the snap of the ball. It is an assessment that does not predict the future but informs the coach on what might be adjusted to help create future success. Final scores are not printed after the first quarter or after practice in the middle of the week.

Teachers, when you label an assessment as formative or summative before using it, you lessen its value. **Every assessment is both formative and summative**. It is how you use it, not what you call it. A good coach makes adjustments after every practice, after every game, after every season. He uses what he knows to make corrections. This is using an assessment formatively. A good coach also understands that every game matters. Using a game this week as a tune-up for a game in the future is a recipe for disaster. Good coaches expect the best from their players at every practice and at every game. It is through this mindset of all things being equal that a belief in the accuracy of results can come, which then allows for honest correction.

In your classroom, ask yourself, are you sending a message that some assessments matter more to students? If you are calling some assessments formative before even seeing the results, have you already diminished their value and their ability to give you reliable data to make adjustments from? If you are calling some assessments summative, are you already indicating that no matter the results, you will not be making adjustments or provide new opportunities for improvement? In your school, are you giving assessments to students three times a year just so that those who wear suits and work in cozy offices can use their crystal balls to predict future success, therefore completely diminishing your ability to use that data to change the future?

In our classrooms, we must work to assess kids regularly. Every question we ask, every assignment we give is an opportunity to assess students. They are all opportunities for students to demonstrate mastery and for us to make adjustments. It is up to us to prove that we know our kids and that we can fine-tune our instruction based on evidence. If we don't, then we can't be surprised when the suits show up with bubble sheets and number 2 pencils asking for more.

6

SIMPLE ASSESSMENT FIXES

Enough metaphors. How do I do this?
Well, there will be more metaphors, but there will also be some fixes.

Alright, we have talked a little bit about the big picture. We've discussed the lens we should use when analyzing standardized test scores. We have discussed how we should define assessment and use every opportunity to collect student evidence of learning as both formative and summative. We have discussed how to more accurately measure student understanding with our grades, but what in the world does all of this look like in a classroom? This chapter is devoted to providing some practical strategies for any teacher, from kindergarten through higher education, to use in class this week. Please don't look at any of these strategies as silver bullets. None are THE answer, but each may provide an answer. Use what you read about here as a springboard to your own thoughts and solutions. Chapter 6 is here just to get the ball rolling. I hope it helps.

Let's begin by imagining that today is Wednesday. You have spent the last two days teaching a new unit to your students and anticipate a quiz on Friday (This is what you always do. Teach Monday through Thursday and assess on Friday). The quiz you are preparing for your students is a typical paper/pencil assignment. To make grading easier, you determine to make your quiz 10 questions long (it's just easier to calculate percentages that way). Every question wrong drops 10% off the final grade, no calculator required. This was the way I organized my own classroom for a few years. In my mind, it worked. I was able to stay on schedule. I could document learning every week to meet my principal's expectations for me, and I didn't have to spend hours all weekend long grading assignments. If this is what you currently do, I am the last one to judge. It was my reality too. However, just because it is what you currently do, does not mean it has to be what you always do. There are baby steps we can take. Remember, right now, we are just providing strategies to get the ball rolling. Later on, we will discuss some of the struggles with this kind of strategy, but for many, this may be a great first step.

I have been to meetings before to help me break bad habits and addictions. The first step is always admitting that I have a problem. If the story I just described reminds you of your own classroom, and if you read the first five chapters of this book and realize it may be time for a change, then you are ahead of the game. You are ready to take your first step towards using assessment to improve student learning, not just to measure it.

__Here is what I want you to try next week__. This is not going to be ground breaking. I am not going to ask you to stop giving your ten-question quiz on Friday, well, at least not yet. Right now, our focus is on using that quiz to help plan for future instruction instead of simply serving as a capstone for past instruction. What we are going to do is break down your ten-question quiz into three parts, one that focuses on the past, one on the present, and one on the future. When I was a classroom teacher, I would typically write my quiz the day before I gave it to my students. The questions simply came from my notes and were the highlights of whatever it was I taught. They were not developed before the unit to serve as the guide posts, but instead, I created them only after I was able to look back and analyze what content I had covered. All ten questions on my quiz would have come from this. It was the capstone on the week we were in.

On your ten-question quiz, instead of creating ten questions that all focus on the current week's instruction, I want you to only ask six questions relating to the content taught this week. Perhaps you had one learning target or one standard that was the focus for the week, or maybe you had six standards, and six targets. That is not really the issue, yet. Whatever it is you taught, I want you to identify six questions that you can ask to determine student understanding for the current week. This will be your focus on the present. Then I want you to identify two questions you can ask that will allow you to determine whether or not students have endurance of knowledge. Pick a topic taught two or three weeks ago and create two questions that will allow you to see if students still remember what they learned from the past. Then for your final two questions, you got it, we are going to think about the future. I want you to create questions about what you are going to teach next week.

Your quiz will look like this:

- 6 questions about present learning
- 2 questions about past learning
- 2 questions about future learning.

I call this spiraling. To make it easier to analyze, I've actually encouraged teachers to print this quiz on two sides of a paper, the six questions regarding the present on the front, the other four on the back.

**SIX QUESTIONS ON THE CURRENT WEEK'S CONTENT
(PRESENT)**

1.

2.

3.

4.

5.

6.

**TWO QUESTIONS ON PREVIOUS CONTENT
(PAST)**

7.

8.

**TWO QUESTIONS ON NEXT WEEK'S CONTENT
(FUTURE)**

9.

10.

Doing so will allow you to more accurately analyze results and make the necessary decisions as a result. From here, you can begin to make inferences about whether or not you are teaching for mastery and endurance or if you are teaching for short-term recall. You can begin to determine whether or not students have sufficient background knowledge for upcoming instruction or whether a review will be necessary. You can determine whether or not students have a solid understanding of this week's learning, whether they retained what was taught, and if they have any exposure to what is going to be taught.

Teaching a Math unit on multiplying fractions? Give students six problems to assess this skill. Then perhaps there are two problems based on the prior unit on multiplying decimals, and perhaps two more questions on the next unit asking students to determine the area of irregular shapes.

Teaching a Social Studies unit on The Civil War? Give students six questions connected to major themes of the war. Then perhaps ask two questions about the unit on the Bill of Rights from earlier in the year and perhaps two more questions about Reconstruction.

Teaching a Reading unit on finding the theme of a fictional text? Ask students six questions about various characters and the lessons they learned from the emerging conflict. Then perhaps ask two questions about the topic of plot that you previously taught, and then perhaps have students identify a similar theme from a non-fiction article that will be discussed in the future.

You get the idea. This can be done in any subject area, in any grade level.

I often talk about the power of 80%. If you hold onto the practice of using percentages in your grading, striving to get a student to reach 80% accuracy is a noble goal for identifying mastery. An 80% in most schools would be classified as a B or B-. Some would argue this is "above average." I would simply argue, it is a lot better than a coin flip. It is safe to say that when a student can identify with 80% accuracy that he can articulate understanding, it was not simply guesser's luck. When grading a quiz that is spiraled, it is wise to create three sub scores, one for the present, one for the past, and one for the future.

The questions on the front of the page help you identify mastery of what was taught this week. If a student answers 5 out of 6correctly, he is a master (this is 83%). Analyzing the items on the back of the page allows you, as the teacher, to determine what comes next. By analyzing the questions on the back regarding past instruction, you can determine if students have retained understanding, lost information, or acquired new learning. Some teachers use these two questions as a retest. If a student did not earn a 5/6 previously, but is now able to get a 2/2, he now gets full credit by proving mastery. If students regress or demonstrate later on that they no longer maintain understanding, as the teacher, you can use this data to plan for review, bell work, homework, practice, etc.… Typically, I suggest, these two problems should not be used in a student's grade, unless they are used to demonstrate new mastery. Adding any scores from the back to scores from the front of the page will simply cloud your analysis.

Likewise, as a teacher, you can use the two questions about the future to help you generate your plan. If students are showing mastery prior to your instruction, do not make them play school for a week and endure your teaching. If they already "got it," then they "got it." If you can determine that students have an understanding of one of the two topics, then you know where to focus your time and energy. You may be able to identify individual students who have previous mastery and who are able to assist or accelerate, or you may find an entire class with no background knowledge helping inform your instruction going forward, as well.

Spiraling assessment is a great first step towards using assessment both formatively and summatively. It is a great first step towards using assessment to plan for instruction, not simply to end instruction. Spiraling assessment is a great way to create conversations among teachers using data in a way that is not threatening by focusing not just on current instruction, but being able to analyze past trends and discuss future plans. It is a first step, but it is not the end. Mastery, after all, is the goal. Teaching students content and skills that last beyond the classroom is what we are all after. Unfortunately, one assessment on one day will probably not be enough for any of us to reasonably attest with assurance that any of our students have true lasting learning.

Most of us don't get the opportunity to teach the same students year after year. We don't have the luxury to follow them into the "real world" to determine if what we taught actually took root. At the secondary level, we may only see a student one hour a day. If we are lucky, we may get to see that student for 180 days, but for others, we may only get to see that student for a semester. At the elementary level, we may get to see each student for seven hours a day, but following up on a student into their "real world" is even more daunting as that future is even farther away. Despite these constraints, I still believe we have the power to measure for mastery. Remember, assessments are not valid or invalid; only our inferences are. It is up to us to create circumstances that allow us to draw the most reasonable conclusions possible with the conditions we have. We can't just use our circumstances as an excuse. It is up to us to figure out how to make sense out of the information we can collect. So, how do we determine whether a child, whether she is five or fifteen, is a master? Well, we can do so with a strategy that is a lot like a game we all used to play as kids.

TIC TAC TOE

I am a runner. I recently ran in the Chicago Marathon. I ran for 250 minutes, 26.2 miles around the city, and 18 of its amazing neighborhoods. I am not fast by any stretch of the imagination, but I am proud to say, "I beat more than 3,000 Masters Runners." Yup. I sure did. Ok, I got beat by 21,000 other runners, but I also finished ahead of 25,000 "regular" runners. That's cool, but the real bragging rights are that I beat some Masters....well, not really. You see, in the running world, a masters runner is just someone over the age of 40. It isn't an indication of talent, stamina, or speed. It's all about age. So even though I finished in the middle of the pack, thanks to semantics, at least among runners, I am a master.

Running may be the only place on the planet where I would earn the title "master." Watching popular prime time TV, we can see what it takes to be a Master Chef...nope, not me. I am not a chess Grand Master. I have to really focus to even remember the difference between a rook and a bishop. I have never been in the military, so I am not a Master Chief. Aside from my running experiences, the closest I have ever come to being considered a master was when I earned my MA in Educational Leadership a few years after acquiring my bachelor's degree. But, owning a master's degree is not quite the same thing as being a master of learning.

Lately, I have heard a lot of conversations around the idea of mastery teaching, a conversation that I love and believe in passionately. It is the belief that we identify a standard target for students, we assess regularly, and differentiate as needed to help each student reach the goal. In essence, we teach to mastery. We teach so that students can be considered a master of the skills and content, but what does that really mean? What does it mean to earn the label of a master in a classroom? Does it mean we teach until students reach a designated age? Does it mean students have to outperform their peers? How do we determine if a student is a master? It's really as easy as playing Tic Tac Toe.

In Chapter 5, I wrote about the dangers of using the MEAN and how it is simply MEAN. I have written about identifying the essential learning targets and spiraling assessments. All of these topics come into play when we are working to determine mastery. Let me also state emphatically that teaching to mastery has nothing to do with simply trying to slap another label on a student. In schools today, we are seemingly obsessed with labels. We call teachers distinguished, effective, and highly effective. We call students advanced, at-risk, and sped. We throw labels around like they are badges of honor, when in reality, all they do is hold us back. Our goal is to make sure students have endurance of education, not a new designation or title. We want to make sure students don't just cram for a test and then forget. We want to make sure students hold onto what they learn, that they can apply it in a variety of settings and that they find value in their new-found knowledge.

As you have probably already figured out, I like to use examples we can all relate to when I write, to not isolate any particular subgroup of educators (apparently except for those people who hate figurative language), so let me use the standard teacher observation process as a simple example. It is a topic many of us can relate to as we live it regularly.

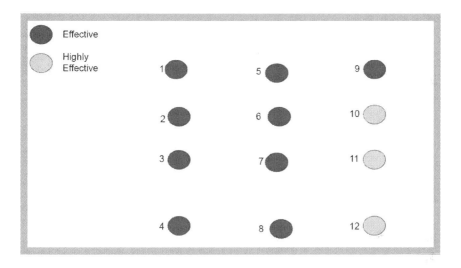

Assume that this year you were observed twelve times by your administrator. This is your assessment of job performance. The first nine times you were observed, you were scored "effective" (this is like a 3 out of 4 on a rubric). After each observation, you were given feedback and coaching so that by the end of the year, your last three observations consistently resulted in "highly effective" (4 out of 4) ratings. If you were a teacher in my building, and I were your administrator, at the end of the year, your designation would be "HIGHLY EFFECTIVE." My job is to help grow teachers, to help each improve his/her practice. By the end of the year, you have shown consistency in responding to the feedback/teaching I have provided, so using observations from the beginning of the year, before my incredible coaching and teaching were provided, against you, just wouldn't be fair. I would never advocate that I should use the mean and just "average" your scores.

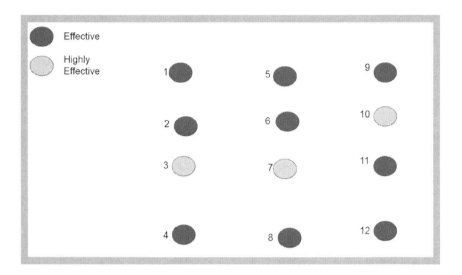

Now, take a look at the image above. Using the same premise, this time, you still have three observations identified as Highly Effective and nine as Effective. Should I draw the same conclusions about your final designation? Have you mastered teaching this year? I would argue, no. There is no consistent pattern. There is no frequency of the results. There is no evidence that what was taught actually endured.

This same mindset can be used when evaluating student evidence. I am a huge proponent of using rubrics and grids to guide student evidence collection. I believe doing so allows each assessment/assignment to be used as a diagnostic to help with future planning and instruction. You can read one of my other books: *It's Like Riding a Bike*, for more information on that. The question always comes up though, is, how many times should a student have to prove he/she can do something consistently to get credit? I say three. You could argue four, five, or a hundred, and I would have no problem with that. Still, I also know that setting such a lofty expectation would make implementation virtually impossible. In sports, the one and done model creates a lot of excitement during March Madness. This time of year is described as madness because during the annual college basketball tournament, it is believed that an upset can happen almost any night. All it takes is one good game for a team believed to be smaller, slower, and less talented to hit its stride and defeat a team that may just be having a bad game. The drama creates a lot of intrigue, but drama is not the goal of classroom assessment. We are looking for a way to document certainty, not flukes. We are looking for evidence that demonstrates a series of success. We want to document what we know about what a student knows.

You may have heard about the "triangulation of data.".This is the idea that we should always use three data points to confirm evidence. State assessment scores should match local assessment scores, should match classroom assessment scores. We should look at three samples, three score collection processes, etc...before drawing firm conclusions. I believe the same is true with student evidence of learning. I call it Tic Tac Toe grading. It's all about getting three in a row.

If in your classroom you are not comfortable using rubric driven assessment, so you give a more traditional paper-pencil assessment/assignment to measure student learning, how many questions must a student answer to prove they understand a concept? Should they answer ten questions? One hundred? All the odd-numbered questions? How about all the even? How many do they need to get correct? Is it 60%, 80%, 100%? If a child can answer nine out of ten, why did they miss one? Does that one matter? When we try to use percentages, we lose out on amazing opportunities.

I believe that when it comes to grading, frequency, and recency matter. I believe it is our responsibility to represent, through our feedback mechanisms (typically grading), what we believe with relative certainty is our assessment of student understanding and mastery. I believe using the power of three gives us a fair amount of certainty to do just that.

Let's pretend I am a Math teacher. If I give my students problems to do in class, I will tell them, "As soon as you answer three in a row correctly, you are done." For some students, this may be the first three questions they answer. For others, they may need more feedback, guidance, and practice. These students may need twenty or thirty attempts before getting three in a row. Both are great as they show consistency and recency. Both sets of students are masters. It doesn't matter when they showed evidence of understanding. Just like a child learning to walk, it doesn't matter how many times she fell down. What matters is mastery of the skill, not completion by an arbitrary deadline that we create.

If you embrace the concept of spiraled assessment presented earlier, perhaps you believe that a student must show 80% accuracy on any given assessment to show understanding. When you give future assessments, bringing in historical assessment items, and asking students to demonstrate that they have maintained this knowledge, three more times, would be great evidence.

Perhaps you are assessing using multiple methods and tools. Students may present their evidence through a project, a test, a debate, a paper, a collage, etc... To help increase your trust in the assessment and to bring about more validity to your inferences, asking students to use three different methodologies during any given unit, marking period, or lesson may give you greater confidence that students understand the topic.

I have shared this methodology with literally thousands of educators. The vast majority think it makes so much sense. The greatest barrier is always the question: "But how does this get translated into a letter grade?"

Trust me, I get the reason behind the question, and I have written a lot about this topic on my blog (https://schmittou.net). For now, though, a great starting point is to simply get a sheet of paper for each student you teach (this may be an entire notebook in high school). Put a child's name at the top of the page. Down the left-hand column, simply list the essential standards you are going to teach this year. Make a grid. Each time you assess a student on a given standard, identify whether or not the student was a master. You can do this with a score of 1,2,3,4. You can do this with a check mark. You can do it with a percentage. Right now, that isn't the issue. Of greater concern is making sure the scores tell you, the student, and the parents something. Remember, your inferences matter more than anything else. Every assessment can be used summatively and formatively. Once you get three in a row...you're done. That child is now a master. Move on. Teach something new. Focus on advancement. Celebrate success.

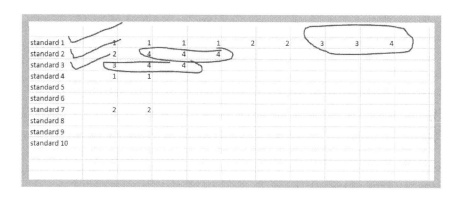

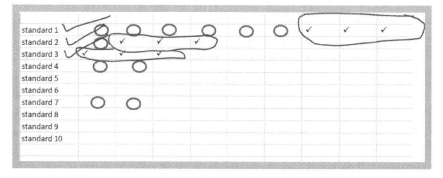

standard 1	65	62	75	77	79	74	85	92	87
standard 2	76	82	84	95					
standard 3	82	93	89						
standard 4	55	62							
standard 5									
standard 6									
standard 7	74	63							
standard 8									
standard 9									
standard 10									

LEVEL UP—RUBRICS FOR LEARNING

Using assessment to document learning is a game changer in the classroom because it helps us not only document performance, but plan for instruction. The next step in our evolution, however, is using our assessment techniques to also communicate progress to other stakeholders, parents and teachers, so that everyone can help in the growth of students. Successful teaching is not done in a silo. Teaching for endurance requires a partnership among the learner and all potential educators, whether they be certified teachers, support staff, administrators, or parents. Everyone must be in agreement about where individual students are on their learning journey and where each is going. Accountability and feedback only work if there is transparency and trust.

How many times have you heard classroom teachers tell their students, "You know math isn't for everyone," or "Some people are just creative," or some other excuse to inspire a child to give up? Our job as teachers is to remind our students that learning is hard. It is a struggle if done right. It will cause some bruises, some humbling, some frustration, but it can be done. Learning is a process, and all of us are a part of it. We are all on the journey to learning more and doing more. Our job is to reach out our hand and pick each child up and show them their potential, to keep their eyes on the ultimate goal and not the struggle they are currently enduring. Our job is to use current circumstances to game plan for future success.

Using a rubric of learning is a step in the right direction. Rubrics have been around for decades in education. Many times teachers hear the word rubric and synonymously think *grade requirements*. They create a checklist of tasks or directions and give students points based on their ability to jump through hoops and create a project that meets their specifications. Maybe a child will earn 10 points for having a picture on their poster board. Perhaps spelling and grammar are worth another 10 points on the assignment, and having relevant information in a poster presentation is worth 30 points. I did this in my classroom as a teacher. Back then, I thought it was revolutionary. I thought I was on the right track because I was providing specific guidance and specific feedback. My grades weren't just numbers or letters at the top of a page. They had meaning. They were very clearly aligned to every hoop I wanted my students to jump through. I very clearly demonstrated which affective behaviors had the most value to me. I used my grading practice to send a message about what was important to me. It didn't matter if my final grade was an inaccurate representation of student mastery. It didn't matter if the final grade helped me develop future plans. The only thing that mattered was my ability to take points away when a child demonstrated a work ethic that didn't fully align with the values I found most critical for long-term success.

For example, perhaps I had a student complete a project in class to demonstrate understanding of a major topic or unit. She was asked to present information to the class. At the same time, I, teacher, held onto a rubric in the back of the room and assigned a final aggregate grade of 35/50, because although the student demonstrated a thorough understanding of the content, she may not have had a colorful picture and may have misspelled a few words. The student would get her rubric back and see a score of 70%, C-, written at the top. According to my already described rule of 80, this child, who demonstrated understanding of the content through this assessment, is not considered proficient (reaching 80%) because she did not color in a picture and misspelled a word or two. Back then, it made sense to me. Today, looking back, all I can say is "I am sorry" and vow to help others do better.

I am a firm believer that being a teacher carries with it the responsibility to teach more than content standards. Our goal is to equip students with skills for success. It is important to help students learn how to pay attention to details and to get used to following directions and following rules. I have no problem with holding kids accountable for almost anything you as the teacher feels is important; however, each night, you as the teacher have to go home and make a series of decisions. You must use your reflective tools to help you determine what tomorrow looks like based on today's successes and struggles. You must be able to determine your instructional moves by looking at yesterday's data. You must decide if the kids understood the content you presented. You must decide if you need to reteach. You must determine what you need to re-teach. You must determine who is ready for something new. A teacher can try to rely on her memory of all of her students and every interaction she had with each one. She can try to use her gut to guide her mind, but inevitably somebody, some student, or some encounter will be forgotten. One of the best tools we have to guide our planning is our own gradebook.

When I was in the classroom, the truth is, my gradebook didn't really help me plan. I never really looked at it to determine my next steps. I didn't really see student grades as a reflection of my work, but instead, grades were seen as a reflection of student effort and determination. When parents would ask what could be done at home to help their children improve their grades, I would always answer with something similar to "study more" or "try harder." It never dawned on me that even using the word "improve" in their questions, parents were already responding to my implied subjectivity. They knew that my grades were not objective. They knew that a grade could be "improved" by demonstrating behaviors that were independent of objectively learning material. They had a bias that I shared, that grades represented a status more than a moment. The things I wish I could change by going back in time now that I know better.

Back then, after grading a project, I might look at my gradebook and see a series of numbers from 0-50 scattered throughout. Those numbers did absolutely nothing to guide me forward. I had no clue what students knew by looking at those scores. Even that looking at individual grades of students did very little to inform me on my next steps. I didn't know if a child had a great colorful picture and a perfect presentation in terms of syntax but missed the content or if the student showed that he mastered the content but made some missteps with his presentation. Perhaps the subject matter being discussed in class contained several smaller essential concepts that required varying degrees of understanding. As the teacher, I didn't know what each child knew, and looking at the grades in my grade-book didn't help me, either. As a result, I often found myself making decisions out of convenience, just doing what I thought was best based on my gut instincts, which, as we have already discussed, may not always be what is needed.

I am excited to share that there are better ways to use our grades and reporting tools than what I did when I was a teacher. Teachers today can use rubrics as diagnostic tools, not just records of effort and compliance like I did. Now that I know better, I am hopeful that we can all do better.

Unlike the rubrics of learning that most teachers are accustomed to that are focused on evaluating a task, rubrics for learning can help us assess learning, not just compliance. A rubric for learning is not task specific. A rubric for learning, if developed correctly, can be used on an infinite number of tasks and has a simple purpose, to determine student understanding. They are not created to judge and assign a grade, but to diagnose and provide prescriptive information. Rubrics for learning serve as a tool for the practitioner and feedback to the learner.

Standard:

List the content students need to know (nouns/objects of the standard) along the left column of the below chart.

Identify the verb of the standard and this becomes your level 3/proficient level of the standard.

Levels "1" and "2" become lower level skills on Blooms. Level "4" is a higher order skill on Blooms.

This rubric should not be TASK dependent, but should help assess LEARNING.

	1 (Not quite)	2 (almost)	3 (got it)	4 (advanced)

These rubrics come into play once you, as the teacher, have selected your ten to fifteen Power Standards for the year. You know that different kids learn in different ways, at different times, and with different styles. You know that each standard you have is complex and sometimes difficult to understand. You know that great teachers can take complex concepts and simplify them by breaking them down. You know your job is to take every child where they are and move them to a point of greater understanding. You also know that somehow you have to be able to document where your kids are at all times so that you can make informed, student centric decisions. You know that because kids learn in different ways, there is also the reality that they can display their understanding of content in different ways. The rubric of learning is a great starting point.

In the template above, we use a four-point scale to document under-standing. A four-point scale is helpful for a lot of reasons, but is not essential. You can deviate from this and use three points, five points, or any total that is consistently applied to every standard. Using a four-point rubric helps eliminate the need for a cumbersome letter grade translation that is interpreted in different ways by so many different people and allows the learner and the teacher to see a simple quantifiable assessment of understanding. A lot of schools actually already use a four-point grading scale; we just call it some-thing different: a grade point average. We take student work, trans-late it to a percentage, translate that to a grade, then take the letter grade, and convert it to a numerical value on a 4-point scale. We then use that grade point average to sort and select kids for honor rolls, scholarships, and programming opportunities. We take our subjective grades, translate them multiple times, just to end up with a grade on a 4-point scale that we could have easily gotten to by just using a rubric for learning. Remember, the more translations we make, the more opportunities we have to lose our original message.

The primary purpose of using a 4-point rubric is NOT about assigning a grade, however. It is not about labeling success and fail-ure. It is about assessing a current understanding and diagnosing prescriptive instruction. It allows us to inspire future success rooted in a current reality. It allows us to play cheerleader, to look at a score-board, and remind a student that the game is not done yet.

The last time you took your car to a mechanic, you experienced something similar. Twenty years ago when your car had to go to the shop, you may have wheeled your car into the garage and let a mechanic bang around under the hood until he was able to create an invoice for a dozen "emergencies" that had to be addressed for a few hundred dollars. Not being an expert in automobile mechanics, you were forced to take his word for it and write a check for the full amount, not knowing if what was reported was actually an issue or not. Nowadays, cars are equipped with diagnostic computers. A trip to a mechanic today begins with your car getting hooked up to a computer that, within a few minutes, can pinpoint mechanical issues. This allows a focus on only the specific problem that needs to get addressed, saving you time and money waiting for an expert to adjust everything under the hood to eventually stumble upon a solution. As a teacher, using a rubric for learning allows you to pinpoint what specifically needs to be addressed and what is already working, saving you valuable time and resources, as well.

In my book *It's Like Riding a Bike,* I introduced the following fictitious example of how this may work. Let's assume you have a state standard adopted for your class that reads, "Students will be able to apply the principles of balance, coordination, gross motor skills, and dexterity to successfully ride a bike." As we previously addressed, standards are not just a list of content. They also include a measurable skill. In this case, our standard is not "balance, coordination, gross motor skills, etc." The standard asks that students be able to APPLY these concepts to RIDE a bike. Because you and your team have previously identified this standard as one that requires assessment, you should already recognize the verb as being one requiring high order thinking. We know that by looking at that one verb, our students are all going to be asked to produce evidence that shows they can apply some new knowledge. Using a rubric for learning, application (the verb from the standard) becomes our target. In a four-point rubric, we use our Level 3 column to detail that standard performance expectation, so the word APPLY is filled in throughout.

	1 (Not Quite)	2 (Almost)	3 (Got it)	4 (advanced)
			APPLY ...	
			APPLY ...	
			APPLY....	
			APPLY....	

Application is our standard goal for all kids for this standard, but we understand that not all students will be at this required depth at the same time. It is not adjusted because a student may have a label. A student label may help us select our instructional approach, but remember a standard is only standard if it is standard. Different kids will begin with different levels of understanding. Using Bloom's Taxonomy as a guide (you may also choose to use Webb's Depth of Knowledge if you are more comfortable with it), a level 2 would contain a verb with a lower level of complexity, and a level 1 would be further down the taxonomy. In this example, a Level 2 may involve showing an understanding of the essential concept, and a level 1 may be recall (see chapter 5 for a quick review of Bloom's Taxonomy).

	1 (Not Quite)	2 (Almost)	3 (Got it)	4 (advanced)
	RECALL...	UNDERSTAND...	APPLY ...	
	RECALL...	UNDERSTAND...	APPLY ...	
	RECALL...	UNDERSTAND...	APPLY....	
	RECALL...	UNDERSTAND...	APPLY....	

Detailing the verbs (the student expectation) for the first three levels on the rubric is always the first thing to do when creating a rubric for learning. The rubric allows the teacher to identify what depth of understanding a student can demonstrate evidence of and then allows the teacher to pinpoint future instruction. Teachers can use the rubric to identify where a student currently is with the goal of moving each forward.

The next step in creating a rubric for learning is to try and articulate the WHAT of the standard. Each standard describes an action as well as content. In our example, there are four explicitly stated elements of content: Balance, Coordination, Gross Motor Skills, and Dexterity. These four subjects become the first column on our rubric. They are what we will be measuring as we assess student understanding. They are what students will be expected to apply.

	1 (Not Quite)	2 (Almost)	3 (Got it)	4 (advanced)
Balance	RECALL...	UNDERSTAND...	APPLY ...	
Coordination	RECALL...	UNDERSTAND...	APPLY ...	
Gross motor skills	RECALL...	UNDERSTAND...	APPLY....	
Dexterity	RECALL...	UNDERSTAND...	APPLY....	

In the above example, I have not provided great amounts of detail within each cell. For example, in the "1" column, we only see Recall....Balance. As the teacher, you may decide that the student needs to be able to recite from memory the definition of balance, simply match the proper definition of balance from a list of options, or do other basic recall functions. How you, as the teacher, decide to collect this evidence, or how the student determines to demonstrate it, is up to you. This column, on this rubric, concerns itself with a student's ability to remember basic information. The format of the assessment is not critical. Your goal is to create a process that allows for you to gather evidence that you can make quality inferences from. What matters is your ability to measure student learning and its depth. If you choose to do this as a group activity, you must know where each individual student is. If you choose to do this using paper and pencil, you must decide if this helps you assess the nature of the standard. Determining the modality of the assessment is an amazing collaborative activity among teachers and students as you work to structure assessments that have value and instruction that guides. Keep in mind, it isn't our goal to get a child to be successful at a level 1 level. Our goal is to get them to at least a level 3. This is the standard, regardless of the starting point.

Moving to a greater depth of understanding is not the same as working towards harder work. These rubrics do not measure whether a child is moving from easier to harder work. They are not measuring whether a student can do more of a task or do a task faster. They measure depth.

As a former social studies and language arts teacher, I will be the first to admit that I am terrible at memorizing dates or spelling words correctly. These skills involve low level recall, but are very difficult for me. If I am given dates or words on a page and asked to draw comparisons, to analyze, or to apply information at a greater depth, I can do so a lot easier on most topics than if I am asked to memorize information I may see as trivial. What I can do is not necessarily harder work, but indicates a deeper under-standing.

When a teacher is assessing a student's knowledge with one of these rubrics, it is not essential to first evaluate whether or not a student can perform a level 1 skill before evaluating their ability to demon-strate levels 2 and 3. In fact, I would argue it should be done in reverse. Because these rubrics are to be used as diagnostic tools, a teacher should begin by measuring if a student is proficient at the standard level (Level 3). If so, then there is no need to measure the levels below. If your car is running just fine, you do not need to go to the mechanic and get your transmission flushed. If a child can ride his bike, he doesn't need to be able to explain the difference between a spoke and a sprocket. It is only if a student is not able to perform at a level consistent with the standard that a teacher should begin to assess what a child can do by looking at lower levels on the rubric. We begin by assuming the standard and working backwards. Rubrics for learning are not checklists and are not ladders. Rubrics for learning allow us to use quality evidence to document where a student is today to plan for tomorrow.

As such, there may be a student who can show proficiency earlier than his peers. There may be a student who can show evidence of mastery at a level 3 level before any classroom instruction even takes place.

In the past, teachers I would have used a student like this to help teach other students. I would claim that allowing a student like this to teach and support others would help him really understand the material better. Although this may have been true, I really had no way to prove it, nor was it always fair for students. Just because a child may have a better grasp of a concept than his peers at an arbitrarily chosen date in time should not mean he is given more work and the responsibility to teach others who may be struggling. As teachers, it is our responsibility to help every child grow, including those who may be moving quicker than the others. With a 4-point rubric, we are given some guidance on how to do this.

Once a child has demonstrated that she has a grasp of the minimum standard by providing evidence according to level 3, you as the teacher must decide what's next. Although the best teachers are those who possess Bold Humility, it is an arrogant teacher who believes the only thing a kid needs is the teacher to learn everything. Some kids may have already learned a few things before coming to you. Using Bloom's Taxonomy as our guide again, we have some options.

After we have crafted the first three columns of our rubric, we now need to determine what is next. We could simply look at our list of verbs associated with Blooms and identify a skill that shows greater depth than the proficient level. A secret you will discover when you begin digging into your standards is that this is actually how grade level expectations are written. In most cases, the content stays the same year to year, but as students move within a school to upper grade levels, the standards evolve to embrace greater depth (high order thinking). Typically, you will notice a pattern that shows standards evolving up the Blooms Taxonomy pathways one level per year, with a few exceptions.

Let's look at our example again to see how this might play out. In our sample rubric, students had to apply their knowledge of four concepts. To show their ability to apply their skills, we might ask them to ride their bikes and measure their abilities to demonstrate the four measurable objectives of balance, coordination, gross motor skills, and dexterity. In most classes, we would have some students who could do this skill when it was assessed and some who could not. In the past, most of us would probably have looked at a kid who could ride his bike proficiently and either ask him to teach other kids how to ride, or we would tell the student to begin working on a new standard. Again, there is nothing wrong with that approach, but it is not necessarily helping that child grow. Just because something is good does not mean it is best.

What if we took the verb ANALYZE (a skill higher on the Bloom's Taxonomy pyramid) and asked our students to compare two different bike designs and distinguish between their form and function? What if we had students EVALUATE professional BMX riders and determine who has a more advanced skill set? What if we had students CREATE and DESIGN a new form of transportation that requires all four components of bike riding but in unique ways? Can you see how this would help encourage our kids who have already mastered standards to become innovators and creators? Can you imagine the energy in your classroom as students worked tirelessly to demonstrate they are proficient in a standard so they could then begin to create and design? Assessment can be a motivating force for kids if done well.

In schools all across the country, teachers are taking this new approach to assessment and using it to challenge the instruction they can provide students. What I have seen evolve is truly amazing. I have seen teachers start with a basic 4-point rubric and evolve it into a more complex 8-point rubric using each of Blooms' levels plus a level for reflection. These teachers work with teachers at other grade levels and create a master rubric for their entire department. For example, I was in a middle school where a 6th grade teacher was responsible for assessing the first four columns on the rubric to get each student to a level 3 of application. The seventh grade teacher was then able to make their starting point the level 3 because she knew at least 80% of her students were beginning there (they also believed in the power of 80) and was able to focus on columns 3, 4, 5, and 6 trying to get 80% of her students to synthesis, before the 8th grade teacher jumped in and moved to the last four columns on their master rubric.

This level of complexity and coordination is taking this understanding to a remarkable level. I have seen some schools use these rubrics in every classroom and move away from grading any individual assignments. In a gradebook, teachers can begin assigning scores of 1-4 on each individual learning objective. Some schools hold onto letter grades to supposedly ease the transition for parents and create a new grading scale that converts scores of 1-4 to the appropriate A-F letter grade.

Ultimately how these rubrics are translated into student labels are not the important part of this process. What really matters is how teachers can use this information to enhance the learning experience they can give to students. These rubrics can be used to assess students using an unlimited number of tasks, because it's not the task that is important. We are not trying to determine a student's level of compliance in completing work. We are trying to determine what a child knows so that we can give them more knowledge and increasing levels of depth and rigor.

If you decide that rubrics for learning could work for you and you have a singular project or activity in mind to support a learning objective, stop right there. If this is done correctly, a singular rubric can be used by all teachers responsible for the same standard, regardless of the projects, tasks, or pedagogical style used. As long as teachers are willing to talk and debate openly about what evidence is satisfactory to demonstrate understanding, there are no limits.

At the end of a school year, a teacher may end up with 10-15 rubrics, one for each standard. These are used to assess all students all year long. As the months and years begin to pass, your expertise in the use of rubrics will evolve and grow as well, showing a greater understanding. Perhaps you started off with ten distinct rubrics measuring ten unique Power Standards, and five years later, you have one large master rubric with fifty embedded skills. Maybe now you are cutting and pasting skills across standards to have units of study that allow you to assess skills from several standards all in one unit. Perhaps you are allowing students multiple redos and retries to demonstrate proficiency and not just relying on one attempt.

Using a rubric for learning derived from a power standard does not just help with Standards Based Grading; it allows a practitioner of knowledge, a scientist, a teacher to become an artist. It allows a teacher to take a look at a canvas and evolve it to grow based off of its specific needs and abilities. It turns assessment into a diagnostic instrument, not a label making machine.

HOW DO WE MAKE SENSE OF IT ALL?

The average teacher spends 100% of her day trying to help every kid be better than average.

Accountability is such an important feature in any person's quest for progress. In my own world, I am beginning to understand my own shortcomings more and more and, as a result, have learned to put people and processes in place to help keep me honest. It's so easy to fall back into old ways of doing things, ways that are destructive and stagnating, but sometimes, often times, easier and immediately gratifying. Accountability helps keep me grounded on what is important and allows me to stay focused on the goals I have established. For example, I often use social media to keep me in check. Those who follow me online know that I post regularly. I document my personal and professional life with as much regularity as someone writing in a daily journal or diary. I do this because I know there are others out there who will see right through it if I try to post anything less than authentic. If I post a picture of myself petting a cat and smiling, they will instantly jump online to call me out as a fake. They know I hate cats (sorry, feline lovers, but I'm a dog guy). If I try to post messages describing my school or district as the land of milk and honey or pretend to live a life free of strife, I have people who will call me out for presenting something that is not quite the full picture.

I have mentioned previously how I love to run, but even there, alone on the streets, I can find myself drifting towards being less than truthful. I need help focusing on what is real. Some people in this world have learned to embrace a concept known as running naked. Now before you get THAT mental image in your head, sorry, I know, too late, THAT is not what running naked is. Well, it is, but that's not what I am referring to here. The naked running I am referring to involves being fully clothed, but free of a watch, no GPS device, no headphones, no technology.

Running naked means running free of distractions. This works for some people, but not me. I need those devices to keep me from lying to myself. When I run, my GPS watch lets me know if I am really keeping the pace I need to. When I run, I can sometimes convince myself of things that just aren't true. Sometimes I coast and take it easy, even though I am telling myself I am giving my all. Sometimes I feel like I have run farther than I ever have before. My body and my mind tell me one thing, but my watch tells me something different. By not running naked, I can take quick glances at my wrist or a quick look at my phone and realize that what I am feeling is not necessarily reality. I may be able to run faster. I may be able to go a little farther. My devices are my reality check.

In writing, in teaching, in living, and in running, I depend on people, processes, and programs to help me find clarity. When I write, my computer monitor lights up with blue and red scribbly marks. Thank God my software program helps me to see some of my errors and thank God for editors and publishers who can freely ask, "Did you really want to write that?:" At home, I have been known to get dressed, look at myself in the mirror, think I am pulling off an amazing wardrobe ensemble, just to then walk down the stairs and hear the truth from my family. I am still not sure why a red and white Hawaiian shirt isn't appropriate to wear to work, but I will trust their judgment.

Accountability helps keep us honest. Remember that old story about the emperor with no clothes. His subjects were convinced that holding him accountable and telling him he was naked only brought embarrassment to themselves. They believed the king knew what he was wearing, or not wearing, and pointing out his nakedness would just make them look foolish. It wasn't until a brave child spoke up and proclaimed the truth that others became more willing to embrace honest accountability as well. The emperor was naked, and he needed to know it.

I think the same thing is true in schools. Some teachers are gifted at teaching naked; then there are people like me, people who are not good at much of anything naked. See, sentences like that last one are the reason why I need editors and publishers. I can't wait to see what they do with this.

Too often, at school, at home, and in life, my gut instincts have led me astray. Perception may be a reality in our own heads, but that doesn't make it real. In our schools and in our classrooms, sometimes we need others to step in and correct our thinking, help us align our inferences, and help us calibrate our analyses.

Sometimes what we see is based more on where we look than anything else. As a speaker, I know I do this all the time. I present to a crowd of several hundred people and focus on the two or three people in the front row nodding their heads, and I believe everyone is following along. We often do the same thing in our classrooms. Maybe we ask one question to everyone in the room and assume the one child who raised his hand and offers up the correct answer was really speaking on behalf of everyone else. We look to our own memories and feelings about how we thought a lesson went to determine if it was a success or a struggle. Again, I am guilty of this.

A few years ago, I was presenting at a large national conference in Las Vegas. I had a packed room, and after ending my session, I was on a high. I felt like I had nailed it. It was one of those sessions where I felt I could have just dropped the mic after an hour and walked out of the room victorious. My emotions were based on hearing my own voice and seeing the crowd through my own lens. Reading the feedback I received a few days later, and reading some of the comments about my inability to stop talking, my refusal to engage the audience, and my perceived arrogance, was the slap across the face I needed to bring me back to reality. Where we look can change what we think and ultimately what we do next, in the classroom and in life. Our gut instincts are not always as accurate as we think they are.

Between Instagram, Pinterest, Twitter, Snapchat, and a thousand other social media platforms, kids, and adults, have become obsessed with taking pictures of themselves and posting them for the world to see. Not just any pictures, though, the perfect pictures. People will hold their phone up, snap a picture, look at the picture's quality and then determine whether it is worthy of being shared or whether another, or another ten, are needed to get it "just right." How amazing would it be if the world actually worked that way? Wouldn't it be amazing if, in the real world, we could actually have countless retakes, could edit our reality to our heart's content, could add our own filters, and crop out everything we didn't like?

In the real world, though, we do not have the option of changing our background. We do not have the option of turning the flash on or off. We cannot choose between "lo-fi" or "Valencia" (my own personal favorite filter is Juno). Often, because of our new obsession with crafting a false image of reality, a fantasy image, a facade for the world to see, that when we face real obstacles, real hurdles and difficulties, with no option to edit, delete, or start again, we do not know how to respond, so we do what I did for so long in my life. We just reject reality and continue crafting a fake image.

Although selfies may be fun for people to take, people need to remember that every once in a while, we must take some time to look in a mirror as opposed to a cell phone image. We must get a real look at who we are and what we are doing so that we can make the necessary changes to improve. The real world is not driven by "likes" and "retweets." We cannot judge our progress through society's impressions. We need to learn to look at what's real head-on and evaluate our own successes and failures.

I could easily take a picture of myself, edit the image to include more hair on my head and a more chiseled jawline, or I could choose to look in a mirror and identify some flaws that I can actually do something about. We all need to be willing to take a real snapshot from time to time, to see an honest reflection of who we are, not just to knock our egos down a few rungs, but to also figure out how to make ourselves better. It all begins with being honest with ourselves. Growth requires honesty. It's as simple as that.

We all work hard every day, trying to make a difference. I work with some amazing teachers who are life changers. They work hard to create lessons that will last a lifetime, yet they are constantly on the hunt to improve. They are amazing because, despite their hard work, they still think they can do more. They create what they believe to be amazing products, then go home and reflect on how to make things even better. Reflection is not a personal action. You cannot do it without assistance. In order to look at yourself, you need a tool.

As I am typing this, I am trying to think about what I look like. I cannot see my own eyes, my own chin, my ears, or my scratchy facial hair. I could go find my daughter and ask her what I look like, but I know she would probably use some objective words describing my height or hair color. She is so sweet, she would shy away from any subjective language, knowing it could hurt my feelings. I could go ask one of my sons to describe my appearance, and I know I would probably get a much more colorful description, including words like bald, weird, or ugly. I could also get up, find a mirror, look into it myself, and form my own descriptions and opinions, based upon my own lens.

In our houses, we all have mirrors that I am sure we look at daily. Mirrors are standard in American homes. We depend on them to assess how we look. But a mirror is not the only tool we use to judge our appearances.

In my own home, I also have a personal scale. I use it not only to assess my health, but I believe that staring at the numbers each morning also helps me analyze how I look. Each morning, as I am getting ready, I look in the mirror and then also step on the scale. I have a mirror and can see what I look like, but I also feel the need to step on a scale and get a different assessment. There have been many days when I think I look good according to what I see in the mirror, but the scale tells me something different. These days, for some reason, I find myself siding with what the scale says. I tend to believe that if the scale says I have added a few pounds that I need to lose them, regardless of what I see in the mirror, or even what other people may tell me.

At my schools, I am always asking my teachers to reflect on something. Some people attempt to reflect while all alone. Some people find a friend and confide in them. In our own worlds, we have to get comfortable taking a good look at who we are through multiple lenses, not just what we see when we look at ourselves, but what others see and what objective tools may tell us as well. Reflection, honest reflection, is the key to improvement.

At my schools, I sometimes see my role as being a teacher's "scale." I know that at times when we look in the mirror, we see what we want to see, whether it is good or bad. We are free to use subjective interpretation to assess our value. I also think it's important to balance that with an objective measure. We sometimes need validation and feedback from an unbiased data point. Sometimes we need a mirror, and sometimes we need the scale. Often, we need both. Sometimes what you see in yourself is more important than what others see. But sometimes your own feelings can sway what is real.

As professionals, we need to put as many tools in our reflective tool boxes as possible and then decide what to do with what we see. Do we just need to straighten our hair, or do we need to put forth the work of losing a few pounds? Should we just smile and appreciate the hard work already invested, or is there more to be done? Find your tools, reflect on what you see, then keep working to improve.

Assessment is not always about creating your own process to measure what you taught. Assessment can also be an amazing reflective tool. Sometimes, we need to look to others and get their impressions and views of reality to help us more accurately determine fact from fiction. Enter standardized tests and evaluations. I know they both get a bad rap from most of us, but they can both actually have some value, if they are understood, and if they are used appropriately.

STANDARDIZED TESTS

Don't get me wrong. I completely understand the frustration so many feel when they think about standardized tests in our classrooms. The administration of these tests, created by the so-called experts, far removed from our classrooms, with no relationship with our students, requires so much time and energy. We have so many things we could be doing to actually teach our students, but instead, we find ourselves passing out number two pencils, removing posters that could be potential cheating hazards from our walls, adjusting daily schedules, and adding additional anxiety and stress just to please bureaucrats and legislators. At least this is what most of us feel.

Why do we spend so much time, energy, and money giving such high stakes tests to kids? Well, the answer is actually pretty simple--trust. For those who may be reading this book in chunks, let me repeat something that was written back in chapter 5 because I think it is relevant here as well. The reason we have so many high stakes tests in schools today is because people, often bureaucrats working in state capital buildings, believe that we need an honest and accurate assessment of what our students can and cannot do. This sounds reasonable enough. The issue is that often in classrooms, how, when, and what we assess does not match up with these so-called "high stakes tests" requested by "experts," and so we feel a disconnect and tension. As a result, those same bureaucrats come back into our schools, through legislative action, and ask for us to administer even more tests so that we can get earlier and more frequent progress updates, or in some places, predictors of future success. In other words, we ask students to simply take tests to predict their success on future tests. There are some assessments available that actually use their ability to correlate and predict future performance as a selling point.

In schools everywhere we have been conducting, what I believe to be, educational malpractice. We have decided to label kids, label schools, and label districts as a result of a computer algorithm. We have taken quantifiable data, entered it into a computer, a computer programmed by humans, so that we can then predict future success or failure, and we don't give it a second thought. We do not question the reliability of these predictions. We do not ask for evidence that these simulations will reflect actual long-term results. We take it at face value that a student identified as "not proficient" will be "not successful."

I am not going to get into the debate about whether assessment results should lead to student grade retention or teacher dismissal. I am not going to get into the debate about how ridiculous it is to have career politicians applying their often erroneous thinking into crafting destiny changing legislation as a result of data they do not understand; however, to be fair, most of us who live and work inside schools as career educators don't really understand what the results of most of these assessments mean either. Part of that struggle is a result of feeling like it doesn't matter. When we are told what the results mean, what the ramifications will be, and what we need to do about it, we feel that there isn't really a need to make sense of any of it. We just go along for the ride and complain about it later.

But, what if we did understand it all? What if we actually did find a way to make these assessments useful? What if we could actually find a way to incorporate the "big data" into our daily instructional planning? What if we could create our own inferences and use our own knowledge to help inform the policymakers instead of allowing directives to always flow downhill? What if?

It is important to understand that not all tests report information the same way. I know, it sounds obvious, but it's not. How results are reported often plays as large a role in the task of drawing inferences as does what is actually on the assessment. In the world of assessment, there are primarily two major reporting categories. There are assessments known as criterion-referenced, and there are those known as norm-referenced. Knowing the difference, and knowing the limitations of each, is a critical requirement for making sense of the results.

I am five feet, ten inches tall. This puts me in the 61st percentile among all men in America. Letting you know I am 5' 10" tall gives you a reference point using a standard measurement. If I am attempting to ride a roller coaster at a local amusement park that has a height requirement of 48," we know that my 70" (5' 10") height qualifies, and I get to ride. I met the criteria. This is criterion-referenced. It is measuring success against a predetermined standard.

Knowing that my height puts me in the upper 39% of all men in America allows me to compare myself to others. In this case, I am taller than what is normal. I am above the norm. If that same amusement park advertised that only people who were "above average" could ride, determining qualifications would be a little more time-consuming. I could compare myself to those standing closest to me in line. I could compare myself to everyone else in my family. I could compare myself only to the men around me. I can compare myself to the rest of the country. When we begin to use comparison data (norm-referenced data), things can get a little tricky if we don't fully understand what we are comparing. Comparing results to a small subsection is what most norm referenced assessments do, as well. Because it is virtually impossible to assess an entire population, a sample is usually gathered; their results become the norm, and others are compared against them.

Remember the phrase I have used repeatedly throughout this book, a test is neither valid nor invalid, but our inferences are? This book wasn't written for staff at local amusement parks. They can create their own policies using whatever method they want to determine who gets to ride their rides. This book was written for educators, destiny changers, and mind shapers. Drawing conclusions by confusing or misapplying a test type is a major problem in American schools today. I am convinced it may be the single greatest instructional issue we have, and that is a pretty big claim.

As I have stated, I currently live in the state of Michigan. Michigan, like many states around the country, is working hard to create educational systems that guarantee a lifetime of success by preparing children in school today with the necessary skills for success tomorrow. One of the skills determined by legislators as essential to enduring success is reading and writing literacy. To encourage foundational literacy skills in children, here in Michigan, there is legislation that states that a student who is reading more than a grade level behind his/her peers at the end of 3rd grade is subject to repeat 3rd grade.

Again, I am not going to argue the legislation and the ramifications of the policy, but I am going to argue with how these students are identified.

One would think that a simple way to identify these students would be to create an assessment that measures third-grade reading and writing standards and then identify which students are not yet proficient. But, as we who work with children daily know, it's not that easy. The legislators who designed the law, I am sure, had the best of intentions and probably thought we could just draw a line in the sand separating those who "got it" from those who "don't got it," but, that's not how it's done, because that is not what learning looks like. When we look at a skill as complex as reading, we are looking at phonemic awareness, comprehension, decoding, fluency, etc. When assessing reading, we must determine which elements matter most and which deserve our focus. When determining how to interpret grade level reading, we must look at state adopted standards as well as subjective bias regarding vocabulary, figurative language, required background knowledge, and even text type (reading cursive vs. Times New Roman vs. social media texting).

Here in Michigan, a year after this legislation was passed, the state department of education has finally determined that the best approach for identifying struggling readers is to create an arbitrary cut score based on a percentile score earned on an end-of-the-year, state-mandated reading assessment. The goal created by the department of education is to not have more than 5% of students statewide qualify for retention each year. Again, I am assuming positive intent here, but using a cut score that takes the bottom 5% of students based on an aggregate score does not help us identify specific areas of deficit, nor does it help us truly understand if these students met the criteria. They have taken legislation that was written based upon an objective measure and created a policy using a normative calculation. Confusing criterion and norms is almost as mean as using the mean, and once again, destinies are in the balance.

In many states, legislators have embraced the idea of focusing on student growth as opposed to a singular focus on student achievement. In the 1990s and early 2000s thanks to No Child Left Behind, many schools and districts began to focus in on so-called "bubble kids," those students who were close to being identified as proficient and with, what was believed to be just a little nudge, could find themselves on the other side of the "got it" line, helping schools receive higher designations and as a result, more funding. Knowing that where we focus we grow, we saw increases in the numbers of students moving above this line, but we also saw increases in the gaps between students as well. We saw students who were on the fringes, both at the top and those on the bottom, showing less evidence of growth and wider discrepancies emerging between subgroups and populations. It is now, as a result, much more common for schools, districts, and states, to articulate plans that focus on the growth of each child as opposed to just looking for a percentage of kids meeting a predetermined cut score, but once again, we have to understand what we are looking at.

When my son Cameron was a year old, his head circumference was at the 95th percentile. When he was two, his head again measured at the 95th percentile. When he was five, it was at the 85th percentile. Now, as a 14-year-old, it is at the 60th percentile. He went from the 95th percentile as a toddler to the 60th percentile as a teenager. Does this mean his head shrunk over the course of the last decade? Of course not. Between his first and second birthdays, did his head remain the same size? Nope. Percentiles do not show growth or regression. They show a comparison to others. They are norm-referenced.

In many school districts, teachers are being asked to give assessments to their students three times a year so that student growth can be measured. Student growth is then being used to help in the teacher evaluation process (we will cover evaluations soon). I believe teachers should be expected to help students grow academically, but I also believe we need to make sure that is what we are measuring. Measuring average percentile scores or comparing growth across populations is a way to calculate growth, but it is not a good way to do it. When we do it in classrooms, we miss so much of the rest of the story, and the same is true when we do it across schools, districts, or states. Perhaps the single greatest danger we have is that so many try to draw causations from things that may only be correlations.

When I present to schools and districts about assessment literacy, I often tell this story. Back in 2015, I moved from Michigan to Florida to work as a turnaround principal. There was a lot to adjust to with that move, but perhaps one of the most glaring adjustments had to do with the difference between the climates in Michigan and Florida. Michigan has incredible weather three months out of the year. From June to September, birds are chirping, the sun is shining, and most days I can get by without a jacket. Florida, on the other hand, has twelve months of amazing weather. Some would argue that July and August are miserable because of the heat, but I love it.

As my family was preparing for our move and discussing the weather, my kids began to get excited and started asking about the possibility of getting a pool at our new Florida house. They were pretty convincing. They talked about the idea of playing together outside all year long, making memories, staying healthy, and genuinely just being happy. I was just about convinced until I started doing some research. What I found was extremely alarming, and as a dad and protector of my family, some of what I found was flat out scary.

It turns out that a few years ago, a study was conducted, and it was determined that in every state in America, there is a correlation between the amount of ice cream kids eat and the number of child-hood deaths resulting from drownings in pools. You read that correctly. The more that kids eat ice cream, the more likely they are to die from drowning in a pool. It may seem like a crazy connection to make, but it is totally accurate. What was super disappointing is that my kids, just like me, love eating ice cream, so as we were preparing to move across the country, I was stuck with a difficult dilemma. My kids were going to have to choose between ice cream and getting a swimming pool.

Some of you reading this may be thinking this is absurd. I agree, but this is what happens when we begin to confuse correlations with causations. We see relationships, and we jump to conclusions. Eating ice cream does not cause drownings, but there is a connection. The connection is actually pretty straightforward. More people tend to eat ice cream when it is hot outside. Likewise, more people tend to go swimming when it is hot outside, so as a result of more people eating ice cream and more people being in pools, there is a greater likelihood of accidental deaths by drowning. There is a correlation between the two, but there is no causation.

In so many classrooms and schools today, we look at correlations and draw conclusions framed as causations. Johnny failed his test on Friday. It's because he didn't study, or maybe we didn't effectively teach so he saw no relevance, or maybe he processes orally better than visually, or maybe he didn't get much sleep last night because his dad was out drinking again, or maybe his dog ran away this morning, or maybe he was just totally bored and didn't feel like taking another test.

In Mrs. Jones's class at the end of the year, her students showed an improvement in their growth percentiles, but Mr. Smith across the hall showed an even greater increase. Mr. Smith is obviously a better teacher, or Mrs. Jones had students who began the year more advanced and therefore had less room to grow, or the students in Mr. Smith's class all had a teacher the previous year who planted amazing seeds within them by equipping them with foundational knowledge that started to bloom this year and the students in Mrs. Jones's class didn't have the same experience, or on the day the assessment was given to the students in Mrs. Jones's classroom, the air conditioning wasn't working, and students were distracted by the climate while those in Mr. Smith's class were residing with a cool 72 degrees environment.

It's not to say that correlations do not ever lead to statements of causation. They can and often do, but creating universal policies based on data that is correlated can be dangerous. Teacher layoff and dismissal based on student growth percentiles is one such example. Using correlations to determine program effectiveness is another. Simply because we see patterns does not necessarily mean there is a clear line of causation. Think about all of the factors measured by John Hattie in his meta-analysis (2009). What he determined is that of the 252 influences on student achievement, only 17 had a negative impact. In other words, most things we do in schools work (93% of all influences studied had a positive impact). Trying to pinpoint through any one assessment or any one tool, what one thing is making the biggest difference for student learning in any one classroom is almost impossible with the amount of time we typically have to make our decisions and inferences. The bottom line is, most things we do in schools are good. Most result in student learning. If we really want to determine if we are spending our time and money in the right places, we have to make sure we are using the right instrument and the right reports. Simply seeing a relationship is not enough.

EVALUATION

Along with student accountability and assessment, America's schools are a place consumed with adult assessment as well. Once teachers pass their initial certification exam, they will rarely be asked to sit down and answer test questions to prove their understanding of pedagogy and content knowledge, in the traditional sense again, but they will still be assessed regularly. Their assessments will primarily be performance-based assessments rooted in observational evidence.

Evaluation will typically involve an expert of education, rewarded with the title of administrator, principal, or dean, observing them in their craft and then providing subjective analysis based on objective evidence that will be collected. The concept is great and holds tremendous promise if we keep a few things in mind.

Imagine, if you will, a situation where an author writes a book. He works hours at a time, preparing his words to deliver a message that will hopefully transform a generation. His book is guided by an editor who gives detailed feedback on the syntax used, the semantics selected, and the style that has been chosen. A publisher then analyzes the final product and looks to identify the best way to get the book into readers' hands to make the biggest possible impact. If the book is a flop and nobody buys it, nobody is transformed by it, and nobody is begging for a sequel, it would be fair to say the blame goes beyond just the author. The editor and the publisher both contributed to the lack of quantitative success. Similarly, if that same book finds its way to the top of the charts and is being read in every state and multiple countries, all should be rewarded, and each involved participant should receive credit.

In today's schools, teachers are working hard to craft lessons that will change lives. They are working to create plans that will inspire and leave a lasting legacy. Many schools have coaches who are tasked with providing guidance and support, while administrators are afforded the opportunity to give feedback and evaluative analysis. It would be fair to say that when things go well, all should get the credit, but when things go poorly, well...in many schools, credit is equally distributed, but blame is often singularly placed. Observations, and the related evaluation process, are simply a form of assessment. Administrators must use the evaluation process formatively just as a teacher uses classroom level assessments. It must be used as a reflective tool, not just a gotcha instrument. In too many schools, evaluations are only used summatively, and as a result, there is no shared ownership, accountability, or true collaboration. Every lesson we have learned about classroom-level assessment applies to teacher evaluations as well.

Assessments serve as that reflective lens to help confirm or dismiss our gut instincts. Just as a standardized test can help serve as a check and balance to the data we have already collected, if done right, observations from trusted peers, colleagues, and supervisors can help us grow as well, but the key is the process must be rooted in trust.

Over the last ten years, in conjunction with the standards-based movement, there has been an increased focus on the teacher evaluation process. In my current district, our teacher evaluation process is rooted in the Charlotte Danielson Framework and her 22 indicators of quality teaching (1996). As a school leader, my job is to help teachers, and principals, improve in their craft. My job is to help teach grow as educators, and often my go-to is to provide feedback based on the frameworks of Danielson and Hattie (2010). In my quest to provide criterion-referenced feedback, limited in subjective, norm-based opinions, I try to use research-based standards as a reference point. The struggle is, however, due to the sheer number of standards and indicators referenced by Hattie and Danielson (252 identified by Hattie and 22 by Danielson) my attempt to provide targeted assistance that can lead to true growth, can be overwhelming, both for the recipient of my feedback and me. Focusing on so many standards doesn't work for kids. It doesn't work for teachers either.

Here in Michigan, the law written by state legislators describing the teacher evaluation process is 2833 words long. THAT IS CRAZY! 2833 words to say what I can say in four words. The goal of teacher assessment (evaluation) should be to "HELP MAKE TEACHERS BETTER." Evaluations must no longer be something we, as leaders, do to teachers, but must return to being something we do with teachers. We must help teachers focus on the focus and eliminate all of the extra (stuff) that gets in the way. In my district, we have adopted the mindset that what we do, they do. If we want our teachers to focus on the focus and to only assess what matters most, we must do the same as the adults, and provide feedback and support on the things that matter most.

In education, we tend to make a lot of decisions based on incomplete data. We don't understand quantitative data, so we confuse correlations with causations. We don't have time to read scholarly journal articles, so we resort to looking at graphics placed on social media sites that proclaim to summarize the findings. This has been done with Bloom's Taxonomy of Learning, Hattie's Visible Learning, and Danielson's Framework for Teaching. The proof of this is right here. The book you are reading is available because of this truth. Trying to make sense of so much research can be confusing and time-consuming, so we look to others to try and simplify and summarize. This is actually the very nature of my job. It is actually every educator's job. We are charged with taking the complex and making it seem simple. Sometimes our quest to do so distorts reality, but sometimes it can actually make things easier to manage.

An approach we use in my current district is an example of trying to make the complex more manageable. This is an approach, not the approach. When you read what we do, please do not take this as an edict that all must follow. This just happens to be what works for us. I am hoping that our process provides momentum for others, but it is not necessarily a script that must be followed. As was stated, the Danielson framework describes 22 characteristics of quality instruction. The framework does not rank and sort any of the characteristics based on value, but simply outlines what quality instruction would look like based upon 22 research-based standards. Similarly, John Hattie has identified more than 250indicators, or drivers, of student learning. He has ranked these indicators by effect size and has described which actions have the potential for the maximum impact on student achievement.

By looking at the work of Danielson and comparing it to the work of

Hattie, I found that only 10 of the 22 indicators described by Danielson, and listed on our teacher evaluation rubric, have an effect size of greater than .56 (the closer to 1, the bigger the impact). Effect size basically tells us the strength of the relationship between items. It lets us know how strongly items are actually correlated, like ice cream consumption and swimming. Typically, if two items have an effect size of .4 or greater, it is believed that the two items have a strong relationship. Imagine if we used this statistical principle to calculate the effect size of two people before allowing them to walk down the aisle and say, "I do." Game changer, but that is a completely different topic.

Danielson makes the claim that all 22 items on her framework are evidence of good instruction. I agree. But as was stated earlier, almost everything we do in schools is good. Almost everything has a positive impact on student achievement. What we have to do is begin to focus on what matters most. Just like in the classroom, almost everything we teach kids is good. Almost everything is important, but some things simply matter more. In my district, we have decided that our evaluations of teachers will only include the top 10 indicators according to effect size. Our students have Power Standards and essential skills, so do our teachers.

To make it even clearer for teachers, when they are given feedback in a quantifiable manner at the end of the year, the 10 indicators we use are weighted according to effect size. For example, "Using assessment in instruction" will be multiplied by its effect size of .9 while "Selecting instructional outcomes" will be multiplied by its effect size of .56. We focus on the focus with our feedback and our assessment because we want to focus on the focus with our instruction and our coaching. We may give guidance and have discussions about other elements of teaching and professionalism, but these teachable moments will not be things that we formally assess. For example, if a teacher decides to wear jeans or yoga pants to school every day, we may have a conversation, but this will not impact her final evaluation score. Another teacher may spend hours every weekend rearranging her furniture and bringing in a variety of flexible seating options. I may love this, but again, no quantifiable impact on the final evaluation score.

FRAMEWORK FOR TEACHING EVALUATION	1	2	3	4	Score	Hattie Effect	Weighted Score
1c. Selecting Instructional Outcomes					▼	0.56	0
1d. Demonstrating Knowledge of Resources					▼	0.77	0
1e. Designing Coherent Instruction					▼	0.57	0
1f. Designing Student Assessments					▼	0.9	0
2b. Establishing a Culture for Learning					▼	0.72	0
3a. Communicating with Students					▼	0.75	0
3d. Using Assessment in Instruction					▼	0.9	0
4c. Communicating with Families					▼	0.73	0
4d. Participating in a Professional Community					▼	0.62	0
4e. Growing and Developing Professionally					▼	0.62	0
Remaining feedback indicators							
1a. Demonstrating Knowledge of Content and Pedagogy					NA	0.09	NA
1b. Demonstrating Knowledge of Students					NA	0.23	NA
2a. Creating an Environment of Respect and Rapport					NA	0.41	NA
2c. Managing Classroom Practice					NA	0.37	NA
2d. Managing Student Behavior					NA	0.19	NA
2e. Organizing Physical Space					NA	0	NA
3b. Using Questioning and Discussion Techniques					NA	0.46	NA
3c. Engaging Students in Learning					NA	0.44	NA
3e. Demonstrating Flexibility and Responsiveness					NA	0.33	NA
4a. Reflecting on Teaching					NA	0.32	NA
4b. Maintaining Accurate Records					NA	0	NA
4f. Showing Professionalism					NA	0	NA

Name: School: Date: Position: etc. that d

By helping our teachers focus on the focus, we are trying to help them prioritize, to get out of the weeds, and really place an emphasis on what matters most. Just like with Standards Based Instruction, a teacher can still introduce topics to students that are not a priority; they simply will not grade and assess them. The same is true with teacher evaluations. Principals are free to have conversations about professional dress, about meeting deadlines, and about writing learning targets on the board, but they just don't include these as a part of the formal teacher grading/evaluation process. As we all know, what we grade is what we value and what we value is what we teach.

In my district, we are committed to not only helping our students focus on what matters most, but we also want to cut out the red tape and eliminate as many hoops as we can for our teachers, and I challenge you to do so, too. After all, if it's all about the students, you better make it all about the teachers. They are the ones who make a difference every single day.

8

WHEN WE GET THE DATA WRONG

Why does this even matter? A grade is just a grade, right?

I know it may seem a little late into this book to finally start discussing why any of this matters, but my rationale is actually pretty strategic. I am a firm believer in assuming the good and doubting the bad. As such, I believe that the vast majority of educational policies that we have in place today dealing with the concept of assessment and data were not put into place simply to ruin the lives of teachers and students. That has simply been an unfortunate byproduct. I believe that most rules, regulations, and beliefs are actually in place as a result of the best of intentions, but good intentions do not always translate into best practice. The first six chapters of this book were written to try and give individual teachers practical strategies to use in single classrooms. I know that sometimes trying to get entire departments, grade levels, schools, or districts to embrace change can be extremely daunting and sometimes paralyzing. My hope is that individual teachers will embrace the concepts and approaches on the previous pages. Once enough individuals begin to experience success, real change can begin to happen. We can then sit down with our own tangible evidence of success and engage in the crucial conversations to help change the systems we have in place. This chapter is designed to help arm you with the tools needed to engage in those conversations and to empower change beyond any single classroom.

GRADING:

Probably the single greatest piece of pushback I hear from educators about implementing any of the ideas presented in this book is: "But my school has a policy that dictates how we have to assign grades to kids. I can't just go against it." These educators are absolutely correct. I have heard from some who say they are willing to buck the system and be a renegade, but I don't recommend it. You can only continue to be a positive influence for kids, if you are still there to be a positive influence for kids. Few things drum up debate and controversy in a school like a conversation about grading. This is because grading is about so much more than simply providing feedback based on mastery. It is a conversation about values and priorities. It is a conversation about what each of us sees as important. As much as we try to tell our students, "I don't give you a grade. You earn a grade," the reality is, our subjective opinions determine what we decide to give credit to and what we do not. Do you value extroverts over introverts? Do you give points for class participation based solely or primarily on a student's willingness to raise his hand and speak in front of his peers? Do you value arbitrary dates and deadlines? Do you take off points from student work based on when it is turned in? Do you believe student math fluency requires the memorization of math facts within an arbitrarily designated time? Do you believe students should be able to identify various parts of speech in a sentence? Do you believe all students should be required to read one specific novel? Do you believe all students should have to run a mile within a certain time limit? The reality is: what you grade is what you value. That is not a bad thing, but it does create for some stressful conversations. Knowing that having a conversation about grades will in all likelihood go well beyond discussions about mathematical principles, averages, scale scores, and g.p.a.'s, and that it will probably turn into a conversation around personal beliefs, bias, and values is a great awareness to have before you willingly engage in the debate. As educators, we have to constantly decide which conversation to have, which topic to debate, and which hill is worth dying on. Changing how schools provide grades will never be worth the fight if it doesn't also result in a change in instruction and student learning. So what do you do?

Start with questions. Lead with questions. Never stop asking questions. It's that simple. I have made a career out of speaking and writing about my love of Standards Based Grading, but the irony is, I do not think it is THE answer for any school. It is AN answer. Conversations about grading, assessment, and data can have real power if the conversations are rooted in meaning making, not judgement. Allowing these conversations to serve as a springboard to conversations about feedback, assessment, standards, fidelity, communication, and instruction allows for an amazing opportunity for substantive change if we are willing to embrace why we are having the conversations. The conversations should never become so rigid that we debate how we will evolve our grading if we don't first evolve our thinking about why we may need to.

Imagine once again that I am your building administrator, and as a result, I am your primary evaluator. At the end of the school year, I am charged with the task of providing you not only feedback on your performance, but also a label of your effectiveness. I have already mentioned in this book that I am a runner. I run every single day. I am not fast, but can run far. As a matter of fact, as I am writing this, I have run four marathons and, in the past ten years, have run a total of 12,000 miles (yes, I chart my miles in my quest to run around the world, 25,000 total miles). I run because it keeps me healthy. I run because doing so gives me time to think, to reflect, and to plan. I run so that I can have an opportunity to listen to podcasts and audio-books which allow me to grow and learn. I am a firm believer that my running helps me be a better educator. But what if I took that belief and transferred it to you and to every member of your school staff? What if I made the statement that during this school year, a portion of each educator's evaluation would be impacted by that person's ability to run? To earn an effective score, equivalent to being proficient, a teacher would have to run at a level comparable to me. Because I am a distance runner, I place the effective/proficient bar at running 10 miles in 72 minutes. If a person wants to earn a highly effective label or distinguished score, he/she would have to run the same distance faster than I do. Those who are not able to perform at my level will get a failing score. Because I am a nice administrator, I would never just surprise people with this. I would announce this in September and allow each person to train all year with a final running assessment to be held in May. Let me ask you, if I were your administrator and I implemented a plan similar to this, do you think a grievance would be filed on me by the union? Absolutely!!

Some could argue that such a plan simply isn't fair. Some people have never run a day in their life and would have a distinct disadvantage when being compared against a man who has been running consistently for more than a decade. Others may have a physical limitation, a prior surgery or injury, that would inhibit running any distance. Others, maybe the PE teachers, would argue that they finally have a system that has been crafted towards their strengths. Perhaps the claim would be made that evaluating a person's running ability has nothing to do with their ability to deliver quality instruction, despite my claims of it working for me.

I recognize that this example is somewhat ludicrous. Still, I also recognize that similar things happen every day in our schools and classrooms, where we as the adults, look at our students and assess them on things that we consider to be of utmost importance, because it worked for us, even if it has nothing to do with the content we are charged with instructing and assessing. Items such as punctuality, neatness, organization, effort, creativity, etc...could all be seen as critical elements for future success. I could make the claim that taking the time to cut the darn hairy edges off of notebook paper before turning an assignment in is essential for demonstrating respect by eliminating those tiny scraps of paper from littering my take home bag (this was actually something I used to require in my classroom) and refuse to accept any papers that were turned in without this extra step of paper maintenance. I could argue that turning an assignment in late is unacceptable as it shows a lack of priority and attention to detail, and as such, points are deducted for each day or hour it is late. I could list thousands of examples that illustrate things we do every day in our classrooms where we arbitrarily determine what we value and what we don't by what we grade and what we assess, in ways very similar to my desire to assess your ability to run.

Often we justify our actions by claiming that we gave each person ample time to prepare. We justify our decisions by arbitrarily determining a "fair" grade weighting. We give students a final exam, a redundant exam-measuring content already assessed, count that score more than any other score, and send the message that this singular assignment is of greater value than all others. We spend 40 weeks a year offering instruction, guidance, and support, and then tell a student that his/her final grade will be impacted more on his/her ability to study, to cram, to learn independent of a teacher than anything else and send the message of what is more important. We have policies in place that allow students to opt out of exams if they have perfect attendance, sending the message that being present is more important than mastery. We have policies in place providing grades of a zero if a student is caught cheating, therefore using grades as a weapon for discipline as opposed to a way to reflect mastery. When we begin to discuss grading, again, there is no right or wrong way to do it, as long as there is consistency. When we assign grades, we are providing feedback to both parents and students. The grades we assign send a message. Do others know what that message is?

My oldest son is currently in 8th grade. What follows is a snapshot of his grades when he was a sixth grade student. At his school, there are four marking periods. If you were his parent and you received this report card at the end of the third marking period, what would you do?

Period	Subject	1st Marking Period	2nd Marking Period	3rd Marking Period	4th Marking Period
1st hr	Language Arts	B+	C-	C	
2nd hr	Social Studies	A	A	B+	
3rd hr	Math	C-	B-	B+	
4th hr	P.E.	A	A	A	
5th hr	Art	A	A	A	
6th hr	Science	A-	B+	A-	

As his parent, what feedback would you provide? Would you focus on the declining grade in Language Arts? Does this show a decline in motivation or a decline in understanding? Are the same skills and competencies being assessed in the third marking period as was in the first? What will be the expectation in the fourth marking period? Would you focus on his mastery in PE and Art and assume he will get an athletic scholarship for his obvious mastery or apply early for a grant to attend a prestigious liberal arts college in New England, or would you assume these are obviously blow off classes? Would you look at the math grade and celebrate improvement, or would you question how his grade could improve if math skills are supposed to build off of earlier foundational knowledge? What would you do? What story do these grades tell?

Now flip roles and assume you are the school administrator. When I was a building principal, each marking period, I would lock myself in my office and spend a day signing each student's report card. I did this so that I could write notes to the students and send the message that I was aware of this/her strengths and struggles. What message would you write? Would you say, "Keep working hard?" What evidence do you have of work ethic? Would you write, "Great job?" What makes this great?

If the purpose of grades are to communicate progress or mastery, we must make sure our expectations are clear, and our standards are defined. Grades are often a way to summarize multiple assessments. If we work hard to ensure each assessment is analyzed for accuracy and reliability, we must work to make sure our summary of those assessments does so as well. After all, if our grades told the whole story, there would be no point in having parent teacher conferences. If conferences in your school serve as a mechanism to simply explain grades, then what is the purpose of assigning grades?

Does it even matter? Well, let me ask you a few more questions. In your district, do you have a valedictorian? Is your valedictorian selected based off of a grade point average? Is that grade point average determined as a result of every class taken in high school, or does the grade point average take into account grades earned in kindergarten? Why? Are those grades impacted in any way based on what teacher a student has or what classes he/she is scheduled into? Are extra points awarded for taking classes that may have an "advanced" label? Are scholarship dollars available based on a student's rank according to grade point average?

In your school, do you have an honor roll? Is that honor roll a result of grades earned or growth? Do students on the honor roll earn a reputation that is different from a reputation earned by a student with a different label? Does that label in any way impact classes available, expectations, or levels of autonomy provided? Do these labels earned in elementary or middle school have any impact on available courses in high school that may impact possible grade point averages and scholarship opportunities later on? These are big questions with destiny impacting implications, and those implications are not just for kids.

Education is a high stakes environment these days, and it should be. Educators are charged with preparing the next generation of world changers, and we have to take this responsibility seriously. I understand the intent of state and federal agencies, here in the U.S., who want to hold schools and educators to high standards for success. I believe all educators have a desire to do amazing work and to inspire students to find present and future success. I also believe that some educators are further along in their development of having sound pedagogical practices and that others are still growing into their gift. What I have a hard time with is using assessment and evaluation (which are really the same thing) in the punitive way in which it is used in so many schools, districts, states, and countries today.

I have had the opportunity to work in a couple of states and to speak and share in dozens more. Something that is concerning to me is the number of educators who work out of fear, today, everywhere I go. It's not just a fear for their physical safety. It is a fear over their job security. We operate in a system that speaks of embracing failure, that verbalizes the need for innovation, but punishes those who actually do so. This may sound harsh, but it is the reality.

As a father of four kids, I understand what it means to grow into your strengths. When I got married, I longed for the day that I could be a dad. I had visions of playing catch out back. I dreamed about the days of summer campouts and fishing trips. I had visions of grandeur. Five years into my marriage, my wife finally came to me with the news I had been waiting for. She was pregnant, and my dreams were coming true. Although I had the dreams in my head of what being a parent could be, I knew I wasn't fully prepared for the reality, so I made a trip to a local bookstore and picked up a copy of almost every parenting book available. I read each from cover to cover over the next nine months, but the reality was, reading those books didn't really do much for me. The only thing that really prepared me for being a parent was being a parent.

Looking back on it now, those first few years of parenthood were a mess. It's crazy, but I think I am actually a better parent now that I have four kids than I ever was when I only had one. Being able to learn from my mistakes, adjust my styles, learn what's really important, and determine how and when to intervene have all been learning experiences for me, each resulting from prior failures. If only this were the way we treated the career of being an educator today.

Instead, what we have created is a system in which many educators jump into their career after five years of preparation, dreaming, learning, and reading with the expectation of perfection cast upon them from year one. In many places, new teachers are seen as expendable. If results are not obtained in the first year, contracts are non-renewed with new teachers brought in to try again, and teachers who waited their entire lives for the opportunity to change destinies are left on the outside looking in, discouraged, disillusioned, and fearful of ever showing weakness or struggle. In many states, the teacher evaluation process has evolved from one that encouraged reflective feedback, retakes, redos, and vulnerability, to one that no longer welcomes weakness, struggle, or innovation. We have created a system that no longer embraces the growth of educators through trial, error, and experience, and instead, have created a system that looks to teachers and determines if they "got it" or "don't got it." We wonder why we struggle to dissuade this mindset within our classrooms for students.

Just like with parenting, the only way to become better as a teacher is to teach. We reward educators through increases in pay based upon years of experience, believing that time in the classroom results in improvements in practice, which makes perfect sense. Yet, at the same time, we treat novice teachers as though they should have it all figured out the moment they walk through the door. In my previous book, *Bold Humility*, I explain how we need to evolve our teacher evaluation process, so I won't do so here, other than to connect this back to our understanding of assessment.

First, we must believe that student assessment results are impacted by the effectiveness of teacher instruction, positively or negatively. I know many, even after reading the rest of this book will still question whether the standardized tests used in most states and districts accurately reflect what matters most. Still, the reality is standardized tests, for the most part, accurately assess standards. The debate about which standards are being assessed and whether they have value is one you are free to take up, but the fact that the assessments are standardized is a reality. Given this, logically, we should assume that teachers with more experience, and therefore more expertise, would experience greater levels of success. A fun little experiment would be to look at the results in your school or district to see if this logic holds true. In most places, it actually doesn't.

In many schools and districts, we see no correlation between years of service and quantitative assessment results, which brings to question whether we truly have a system that allows for teacher development and growth, or whether we have a system that rewards the compliant and the rule followers. Again, what we do, they do. We can't ask our students to be risk takers and innovators if we cannot allow the same for our educators. It is our collective responsibility, whether a teacher, an administrator, a parent, or a legislator, to understand that teachers will make mistakes. Teachers will take chances. Teachers will grow. Teachers will learn. We cannot fixate on failure. We cannot label early defeats. We need to stop describing teachers by the grades they earn, just as we need to stop doing the same for students.

As I write this, there is a national teacher shortage. Although some may claim it is due to financial limitations, I knew when I became an educator two decades ago that I wouldn't make a lot of money. Teachers have always been underpaid. I am a believer that we have a shortage, in large part, because of how we use assessment to define teachers, to stifle them, and to box them in. In an age when we need the best of the best to be in front of our students, encouraging them to confront the status quo and make the world better than it has ever been, we must allow for our inferences of assessment and evaluation to be open to embracing a growth mindset and encouraging continuous improvement from all, not just our students.

Here are a few questions you can ask: Should teacher evaluation scores be based off of growth or achievement? Should teacher growth be reflected year to year or during the year? Should we have Teacher of the Year competitions, or does this create a subjective lens for evaluation? Is merit pay fair? Do we practice what we preach? Should educators and students be held to the same standard? Are student assessment scores a fair way to assess teacher effectiveness? Again, just like with student grading, there is not necessarily a right or wrong way to address these issues. The conversations matter. The quest for improvement matters. There is no silver bullet or magic pill, but our treatment of assessment has major implications on all we do.

There is a reason data has become the new forbidden four letter word in schools today. It is no longer a way to measure success. We have turned our definition of data into a quantifiable limiting assessment of content, and dismissed all other methods of evidence collection. If we want our students to embrace growth, we must embrace growth. If we want teachers to collaborate and demonstrate life-long learning, we must encourage vulnerability and allow for struggles. Data should never be used as a weapon of mass destruction, but instead as a building block for future development. We dismiss data that harms and embrace that which encourages. The first step towards creating a system that welcomes assessment literacy is creating a system that understands that assessments are not the issue; our inferences, our ignorance, and the way we have used both so recklessly is. I am a believer that if we actually assess more, if we learn more, if we struggle more, if we grow more, we will not only change the future of our students, but we can change the entire system of education. So go forth and assess, assess, assess, but for God's sake, stop labeling and stop judging!

SOURCES

Bloom, B. S. (1956). *Taxonomy of educational objectives: The classification of educational goals*. New York: McKay.

Danielson, C. (1996). *Enhancing professional practice: A framework for teaching*. Alexandria, VA: Association for Supervision and Curriculum Development.

Hattie, J. (2009). *Visible learning: A synthesis of over 800 meta-analyses relating to achievement*. London: Routledge.

Schmittou, D. (2018). *Bold Humility*. Nashville, TN: EduGladitators Publishing.

Schmittou, D. (2017). *It's Like Riding a Bike: How to make learning last a lifetime*. Bloomington, IN: Archway Publishing, Simon and Shuster.

Schmittou, D. Personal blog. https://schmittou.net

ABOUT THE AUTHOR

Having been an educator for more than twenty years, Dave has earned a reputation for being a disruptor of the status quo, an innovator, and a change agent. Having served as a classroom teacher, school-based administrator, college professor, and central office director, he often uses real-life stories and examples of his own life as a father of four kids and the ups and downs of his career to describe why and how we need to confront "the way we have always done it."

He has written multiple books, including *It's Like Riding a Bike: How to make learning last a lifetime*, *Bold Humility*, along with this book, *Making Assessment Work for Educators Who Hate Data but Love Kids*. He speaks, consults, and partners with districts around the country and loves to keep learning and growing.

OTHER EDUMATCH TITLES

EduMatch Snapshot in Education (2016)
In this collaborative project, twenty educators located throughout the United States share educational strategies that have worked well for them, both with students and in their professional practice.

The #EduMatch Teacher's Recipe Guide
Editors: Tammy Neil & Sarah Thomas
*Dive in as fourteen international educators share their recipes for success,
both literally and metaphorically!*

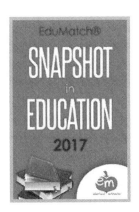

EduMatch Snapshot in Education (2017)
*We're back! EduMatch proudly presents Snapshot in Education (2017). In
this two-volume collection, 32 educators and one student share their tips for
the classroom and professional practice.*

Journey to The "Y" in You by Dene Gainey
This book started as a series of separate writing pieces that were eventually woven together to form a fabric called The Y in You. The question is, "What's the 'why' in you?"

The Teacher's Journey by Brian Costello
Follow the Teacher's Journey with Brian as he weaves together the stories of seven incredible educators. Each step encourages educators at any level to reflect, grow, and connect.

The Fire Within
Compiled and edited by Mandy Froehlich
Adversity itself is not what defines us. It is how we react to that adversity and the choices we make that creates who we are and how we will persevere.

EduMagic by Sam Fecich
This book challenges the thought that "teaching" begins only after certification and college graduation. Instead, it describes how students in teacher preparation programs have value to offer their future colleagues, even as they are learning to be teachers!

Makers in Schools
Editors: Susan Brown & Barbara Liedahl
The maker mindset sets the stage for the Fourth Industrial Revolution, empowering educators to guide their students.

Divergent EDU by Mandy Froehlich
The concept of being innovative can be made to sound so simple. But what if the development of the innovative thinking isn't the only roadblock?

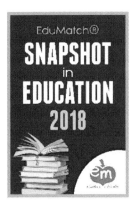

EduMatch Snapshot in Education (2018)
EduMatch® is back for our third annual Snapshot in Education. Dive in as 21 educators share a snapshot of what they learned, what they did, and how they grew in 2018.

Daddy's Favorites by Elissa Joy
Illustrated by Dionne Victoria
Five-year-old Jill wants to be the center of everyone's world. But, her most favorite person in the world, without fail, is her Daddy. But Daddy has to be Daddy, and most times that means he has to be there when everyone needs him, especially when her brother Danny needs him.

Level Up Leadership by Brian Kulak

Gaming has captivated its players for generations and cemented itself as a fundamental part of our culture. In order to reach the end of the game, they all need to level up.

DigCit Kids edited by Marialice Curran & Curran Dee

This book is a compilation of stories, starting with our own mother and son story, and shares examples from both parents and educators on how they embed digital citizenship at home and in the classroom.

Stories of EduInfluence by Brent Coley

In Stories of EduInfluence, veteran educator Brent Coley shares stories from more than two decades in the classroom and front office.

The Edupreneur by Dr. Will

The Edupreneur is a 2019 documentary film that takes you on a journey into the successes and challenges of some of the most recognized names in K-12 education consulting.

In Other Words by Rachelle Dene Poth
In Other Words is a book full of inspirational and thought-provoking quotes that have pushed the author's thinking and inspired her.

To Whom it May Concern
Editors: Sarah-Jane Thomas, PhD & Nicol R. Howard, PhD
In To Whom it May Concern..., you will read a collaboration between two Master's in Education classes at two universities on opposite coasts of the United States.

One Drop of Kindness by Jeff Kubiak

This children's book, along with each of you, will change our world as we know it. It only takes One Drop of Kindness to fill a heart with love.

Differentiated Instruction in the Teaching Profession by Kristen Koppers

Differentiated Instruction in the Teaching Profession is an innovative way to use critical thinking skills to create strategies to help all students succeed. This book is for educators of all levels who want to take the next step into differentiating their instruction.

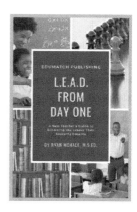

L.E.A.D. from Day One by Ryan McHale
L.E.A.D. from Day One is a go-to resource to help educators outline a future plan toward becoming a teacher leader. The purpose of this book is to help you see just how easily you can transform your entire mindset to become the leader your students need you to be.

Unlock Creativity by Jacie Maslyk
Every classroom is filled with creative potential. Unlock Creativity will help you discover opportunities that will make every student see themselves as a creative thinker.

Make Waves! by Hal Roberts

In Make Waves! Hal discusses 15 attributes of a great leader. He shares his varied experience as a teacher, leader, a player in the N.F.L., and a plethora of research to take you on a journey to emerge as leader of significance.

21 Lessons of Tech Integration Coaching by Martine Brown

In 21 Lessons of Tech Integration Coaching, Martine Brown provides a practical guide about how to use your skills to support and transform schools.

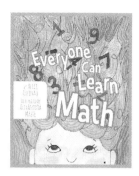

Everyone Can Learn Math by Alice Aspinall
How do you approach a math problem that challenges you? Do you keep trying until you reach a solution? Or are you like Amy, who gets frustrated easily and gives up?

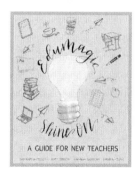

EduMagic Shine On by Sam Fecich, Katy Gibson, Hannah Sansom, and Hannah Turk
EduMagic: A Guide for New Teachers picks up where EduMagic: A Guide for Preservice Teachers leaves off. Dr. Sam Fecich is back at the coffee shop and is now joined by three former students-turned-friends. She is excited to introduce you to these three young teachers: Katy Gibson, Hannah Sansom, and Hannah Turk.

Unconventional by Rachelle Dene Poth

Unconventional will empower educators to take risks, explore new ideas and emerging technologies, and bring amazing changes to classrooms. Dive in to transform student learning and thrive in edu!

All In by Kristen Nan & Jacie Maslyk

Unlike Nevada's slogan of "what happens in Vegas, stays in Vegas," this book reminds us that what happens in the classroom, should never stay within the classroom!

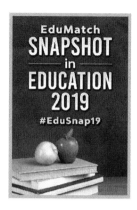

EduMatch Snapshot in Education 2019
EduMatch® is back for our fourth annual Snapshot in Education. Dive in as an international crew of educators share a snapshot of what they learned, what they did, and how they grew in 2019. Topics include Social Emotional Learning, identity, instructional tips, and much more!

Play? Yay! by BreAnn Fennell
Play? Yay! is a book my mom wrote for kids. I'm a toddler, and I like to read. I sit and look at pictures or point to my favorite pages. Do you like books like that? Then this book is for you too! The best part about this book is that you can read it with people like moms, dads, or grandparents. Get Play? Yay! today for fun, rhymes, and the gift of imagination.

The EdCorps Classroom by Chris Aviles
In this how-to guide, Chris Aviles tells you how he accidentally stumbled into the world of student-run businesses, and how you can use them to provide authentic learning to your students.

Strive by Robert Dunlop
This book will get you thinking about how happy you are in your career and give you practical strategies to make changes that will truly impact your happiness.

Thinking About Teaching by Casey Jakubowski

This book explores the thoughts that author Casey T. Jakubowski, PhD has on a wide range of education related topics. Seeking to give voice to rural education, in this unstable time, and reflecting on a wide of research and experiences, this work offers all educators, from the beginning, all the way to the end, a reflective voice to channel their own experiences against and with on their journey.

I'm Sorry Story by Melody McAllister

Do you know what it's like to sit by yourself at lunch? Do you know how it feels when it seems everyone around you has close friends except you? That's exactly how Ryan feels. He wants good friends and he wants to be accepted by his classmates, but he isn't sure how to make that happen. Join him as he learns to put others first and make things right when he has been wrong!

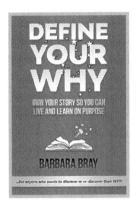

Define Your Why by Barbara Bray
Barbara Bray wrote Define Your WHY from the process she went through to figure out her WHY and through coaching others who did not feel valued, appreciated, or why they needed to live on purpose.

To the Edge by Kyle Anderson
From risks that resulted in immediate success to ones that elicited failure and regret, you surely will be inspired by Kyle's story. Take yourself to the edge and become more of a risk-taker in your life and career!
#ToTheEdgeEDU

Systems, Cycles, Seasons, & Processes by Emjay Smith
Systems, Cycles, Seasons, and Processes takes you on a journey to discover the laws, concepts, and principles that govern the seen and unseen realms of life.

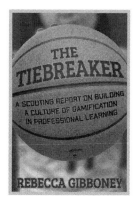

The Tiebreaker by Rebecca Gibboney
In The Tiebreaker, Rebecca Gibboney gives educators the scouting report on how to build a culture of gamification for professional learning.

Fur Friends Forever by LaTezeon Humprey Balentine

Follow this amazing adventure of two dogs with different lifestyles as they take on a new situation that tests them. This story is about friendship and all that comes with it including peer pressure in decision making.

The Perfect Puppy by Kristen Koppers

Many times we often judge others before we learn about them. Abbey Mae learns how it feels to not be accepted by others. Follow her journey as she finds out who she is on the inside.

REAL LOVE by Alexes M. Terry

In REAL LOVE: Strategies for Reaching Students Who See No Way Out,
Alexes uses her personal stories and professional experiences to empower
and equip educators with strategies that can be implemented, immediately,
to support students with diverse needs.

EduMatch Publishing

.

Made in the USA
Monee, IL
27 July 2021